MY
AUTOBIDOGRAPHY

MY AUTOBIDOGRAPHY

PUDSEY

sphere

SPHERE

First published in Great Britain in 2012 by Sphere

Copyright © Ashpen Ltd, 2012
With thanks to Matt Whyman

A CIP catalogue record for this book
is available from the British Library..

Britain's Got Talent is the registered trademark of Fremantle and Simco.
This book is not endorsed by *Britain's Got Talent*.

ISBN 978-0-7515-5087-0

Typeset in Sabon by M Rules
Printed and bound in Great Britain by
Clays Ltd, St Ives plc

Papers used by Sphere are from well-managed forests
and other responsible sources.

MIX
Paper from
responsible sources
FSC® C104740

Sphere
An imprint of
Little, Brown Book Group
100 Victoria Embankment
London EC4Y 0DY

An Hachette UK Company
www.hachette.co.uk

www.littlebrown.co.uk

This book is dedicated to Ashleigh,
my dancing partner,
maker of the finest ham sandwiches
and a companion for life.

A Word From the Pawthor

Yes, it's me. The dog off the telly. One half of the dancing duo, Ashleigh and Pudsey. Some say I'm the most famous four-legged celebrity in the world right now, but I haven't let that go to my head. I might've appeared on the *Tonight Show* with Jay Leno, and attract crowds of admirers everywhere I go, but nothing grabs my attention as quickly as a squirrel crossing my path. Yes, I'm still leading a dog's life, but it's a life like no other. So, when I was invited to write all about it I jumped at the chance. I also turned in circles and possibly also barked a bit, too. Then I stopped to think about it, scratched behind one ear with my hind leg, and wondered how on earth I'd put paw to paper. I'm a dog, after all. We might be able to talk amongst ourselves, like every animal can, but one thing we can't do is write. Can we?

Well, let's just say that there's only one dog who can count Simon Cowell as his BFF. When you're mates with a man who can turn dreams into reality, anything is possible, as you're about to read for yourselves.

As well as my story – from early puppyhood to performing for the nation – you'll get my thoughts and opinions on the issues that matter. Should we fight for the right to have second and third helpings at mealtimes? Why isn't *The Littlest Hobo* on constant repeat? And are dachshunds a pedigree dog or some weird mix-up between a rottweiler, an otter and a squirrel? OK, so maybe nobody has the answers to these questions, but everything I do know I've shared with you here (apart from the whereabouts of Wellingborough's best butcher – that stays with me to the grave). I could've spent my time burying bones in the garden. Instead, I dug deep in different ways, and hope you enjoy the result – which begins on the turn of this page.

Pudsey
Summer 2012, Hollywood

Prologue

Lassie: Never shied away from racing to save kids trapped in wells, but could she have handled Britain's Got Talent? Either way, she's still my number 1 celebrity crush.

I bet Lassie never had to deal with this sort of pressure. The huge television studio was packed with people, and just one dog – me. Even so, I didn't feel completely alone. Ashleigh had carried me like a comfort blanket all the way through the corridors to the wing of the stage, where we waited for our cue.

'Let's go all out for this one, Puds,' she whispered in my ear. 'At least then we can look back knowing we tried our best.'

I looked up and grinned at her. It's my natural expression, so it wasn't difficult to pull off. But Ashleigh only ever had to look into my eyes to see what was really going on. Just then, for her sake as much as mine, I was trying hard to stay cool and calm. This is no big deal, I kept telling myself. A walk in the park. Then I peeked out to get a closer look at the audience, which I admit may have been a teeny mistake. Every seat in the house was taken, as far back as I could see, while the sound, lighting and camera crews were making final adjustments to their equipment. Absolutely everyone present was awaiting our appearance.

In a heartbeat, my confidence vanished.

What struck me with fear more than anything else was the panel in front of the stage, with three empty chairs behind it. Just thinking about who would soon be sitting there to cast judgement on our act made me quiver and shake. Ashleigh picked up on my mood straight away. She rested her cheek on my head and hugged me tightly. Penny, her mum, was with us, and so was Grandma, our lucky mascot. Both put their arms around her.

'Pudsey won't let you down,' Penny said.

'He's a winner,' added Grandma. But all of a sudden I wasn't feeling very sure about that.

We had trained for what felt like a lifetime, and here I was about to make fools of us both. Ashleigh had taken me through our routine so many times, but all of a sudden I couldn't remember the first step. As a result, everything that was supposed to follow seemed like a jumble in my mind. In a few minutes' time, with the judges in place, the stage lights would go up and Ashleigh would walk on, accompanied by one amazingly average non-dancing dog. The audience reaction would be awful, from laughter to jeers, boos and hisses. We could even find ourselves ducking rotten tomatoes if anyone had smuggled them past the ITV security people. I closed my eyes, wishing I was back home watching the show on the TV with the rest of the family. Whose stupid idea was it to audition for this? I thought to myself. Then I remembered. It was mine.

A moment later, one of the show's production assistants appeared behind us with a clip microphone for Ashleigh. Thankfully, it meant she had to turn away from the stage so he could fit it. I found myself facing the fire exit, and part of me thought about scrambling from Ashleigh's arms and making a run for it. But I knew at that moment

I could never abandon her. Even if I was about to make a massive fool of myself, I would do so at her side.

'Ladies and gentlemen!' boomed a voice across the speaker system, silencing the chatter from the audience. 'Recording continues in a few minutes from now, so let's have a big welcome back for the judges ...'

I heard the three names in turn, marked by a frenzy of clapping and cheering, but by then I was focused on just one thing: a cardboard box beside the door. It was tatty and filled with coils of cable, but it reminded me of one I'd found myself inside a long time ago, when my future looked bleak and the thought of dancing on stage in front of millions of viewers was a world away. That was the moment when I knew where I belonged. It reminded me just how far we'd come, the struggle we'd gone through to get here and the challenge we now faced to put in a pawsome performance.

'I love you, Puds,' whispered Ashleigh, and she turned to the stage once more. 'Let's show them what we can do!'

1

Don't be fooled by this picture. I may look
like I'm having a nap, but in reality
I've just tripped over my tail.

I wasn't the last to be born in my litter. Even so, my brothers and sisters still treated me as if I was the runt.

'Get out of the way,' they squeaked at me when it came to feeding time. 'Coming through!' My poor mum was too exhausted by the birth to stand up for me. She lay there in her basket in the kitchen while the others scrambled for the best position. We had been given our first round of inoculations by the vet, and every one of us was declared healthy. Even so, those early days proved to be a fight for survival. I battled to make my presence felt amongst the pack, but it was tough. Fortunately, despite finding myself in the least popular position for each milk round, Mum made sure I didn't go hungry.

'Never mind,' she said, when the others broke off to skitter across the floor. 'You might move about like you were born with four left paws, but I'm sure you'll find your feet eventually.'

My old mum wasn't wrong about many things, but when it came to my coordination she proved wide of the mark. Honestly, I could barely put one paw in front of the other without tripping over myself. That was understandable in the beginning, but several weeks into my life I found it was holding me back. I put this down to being a crossbreed. With a bit of Border collie, some bichon frise and Chinese crested cross in me, it sometimes felt as if I was three dogs competing to control one body. Unlike me, my siblings had it all sorted out from day one. We looked identical, with our shaggy ash-and-white coats and our teddy-bear eyes, but I lacked their balance and quick wits. I tended to sit and watch them tumble and play, rather than get stuck in, which left me feeling rather un-doglike. I wasn't lonely in my litter, nor was I unloved. I was just rubbish at games and a bit embarrassed that I had been born with legs that felt like they each had a mind of their own.

'You know what worries me?' I announced to my mum one day.

'Rabies?' she suggested, which took me by surprise. 'Rabies and fireworks night. It's industry-standard for dogs to worry about them.'

'Actually, there's something else,' I said. 'Homelessness.'

'Shouldn't you just be focused on when your next feed is coming?' she asked as she started to wash me down with her tongue. 'There's no need for a pup like you to concern himself with social issues.'

'What I mean is, when the time comes for us to go I keep thinking nobody'll want me,' I went on. 'My brothers and sisters are all such fun, but I don't have their confidence. Unless I learn to do something clever, I could be cast out into the night and forced to forage out of bins.'

Mum licked my face clean, which stopped me from going on.

'Penny won't throw you out,' she said, and nodded towards the woman who stood boiling a kettle at the kitchen counter. 'She has your best interests at heart. She'll make sure you go to the right home.'

All of us understood, from a very early age, that we would soon be moving on. Mum lived here permanently. As soon as we were old enough, however, my brothers, sisters and I would go our separate ways with new owners, and our whole lives ahead of us.

'Who would want me?' I muttered to myself.

'Oh, I can think of someone,' she said, but left it at that. Then she looked me in the eyes. 'You don't have to be clever to be a dog,' she said. 'Just be yourself and let the real you shine through.'

I clambered out of the basket, catching a claw on the wicker rim as I did so and falling with a thud onto the tiles.

'You make it sound so easy,' I grumbled.

'Oh, it is!' she said. 'And it starts by not fretting so much. Now go and find the others and give me some peace.'

I toddled off, thinking about what she had said. At that age, I wasn't great at multi-tasking. Thinking and walking at the same time proved more than enough, which is why I veered into the table leg. It was all very well trying to be myself, but I was a natural-born worrier. Sometimes it felt like the only thing that I was good at. I gave Penny a wide berth, just in case she decided sooner rather than later that I was fit for nothing but a life on the street. I liked Penny. She was calm, kind and gentle.

Even so, I was convinced that when no potential owner picked me out for a cuddle she would show me the front door.

Until then, though, I was free to roam downstairs in the house along with the other pups. I could hear them tearing around in the front room. They liked to play a game that frankly baffled me. It was called Chase Your Own Tail, but I struggled to see the point. Nobody won. Nobody lost. Everyone just got dizzy. Still, that didn't stop them from playing it all the time. It was as if the existence of their tails kept coming as a total surprise to them, from dawn right through to dusk.

'Watch out,' my eldest brother warned the others when I appeared at the door. 'Here comes an accident waiting to happen!'

'That's very good,' I said, sounding less than impressed while my siblings howled with laughter (they've always been easily amused, even a fly repeatedly hitting a window cracks them up). 'So, what are you up to for the rest of the day?'

My eldest brother looked baffled, as if the answer was obvious, and turned his back on me. 'These tails don't chase themselves,' he said, wagging his, 'and I'm not stopping until I catch mine. Wanna play?'

'Thanks but no,' I said with a shrug. 'That game's a bit overrated, if you ask me. But I'm happy to watch.'

'You don't know what you're missing,' he told me, and raced off once more in pursuit of his backside.

My other siblings continued to charge about in the same way. Though we hadn't been in the world for long,

they had already become much more sure-footed than
me. Keeping well to one side, I observed them tearing
back and forth across the room. At one point, I thought
about joining in, but I knew that if I did I would only ruin
their fun.

It was then, through the blur of my brothers and sisters,
that something caught my eye. The television was usually
switched off during the day. But for once Penny had left
it on, and what I saw was unmissable. A vision I would
never forget. My ears pricked on instinct and I tipped my
head to one side.

'Oh, wow!' I said out loud, but nobody was listening.

On the screen, in a rain-swept street, a man was
singing and dancing. He pirouetted along the pavement,
tapping with his feet as he went and twirling his umbrella
like a baton. Every move he made was brimming with
poetry and grace. For a pup who was constantly tripping
over himself, he had the kind of balance and control that
was out of this world. I watched intently, so spellbound
by the spectacle that I barely noticed Penny return to her
chair behind me with her freshly made cup of tea. She
patted me on the head, a gesture which often made me
freeze. Any time she touched me I was convinced it
would lead to her scooping me up, before driving me into
town and dropping me off on a street corner. Instead, she
sat back with a biscuit, as gripped as I was by this musical magic.

Then, as the song reached a crescendo, my eldest brother
barrelled into me. He knocked me clean off my paws and
sent me skidding across the wooden floor.

'What are you doing standing in the way like that?' he asked. 'If you're going to watch the television, be a lap dog!'

Even though I was splayed out on the floor, my eyes remained locked on the screen until the very last note of the song. That's when I faced him and said: 'Watching television is one thing, but I'm going to star on it!'

He rolled his eyes in response, and shook himself down from head to tail.

'Oh man,' he said. 'A luvvie in the litter!'

'I'm serious!' I drew his attention to the TV once more. 'One day I'll dance like that. Just you wait and see.'

My eldest brother looked around, as if to check that nobody else had heard my declaration. Then he took me to one side, around the side of the sofa. Even if people knew that animals could talk, I doubted that Penny would've backed me up here. I'd hardly shown much promise, after all. At the time, I was about as graceful and poised as a drunk on a pedalo.

'You're a dog,' my brother said, as if I had forgotten, and put his paw around me. 'Dogs don't dance. They dig and bark, eat and sleep. The hardest thing you've got to do is drag your backside across the carpet in a straight line from time to time. That's all you have to master to fulfil the brief, all right? Don't make life difficult for yourself.'

'I can feel it in my bones,' I insisted, and glanced at the television. 'It would be a dream to become a dancer.'

My brother looked me up and down, a grin crossing his face.

'You know what I dream about?' he said proudly. 'Running after stuff. You can't go wrong with a dream like that. It's so exciting!'

'But do you ever catch anything?' I asked. 'Isn't the catch important?'

My brother focused on a point midway between us. He was thinking hard.

'Who cares about that,' he said finally. 'It's all about the chase, baby. Chase, chase, chase!'

'I'm not so sure,' I said, but already I had lost his attention.

'What is THAT?' he asked, looking behind him, first one way and then the other. 'Did you see that? THERE'S SOMETHING MOVING BACK THERE!'

'Um, it's your tail,' I said as he eyed it swishing back and forth.

'Stay where you are. I'll handle this!' he yelled, and promptly pounced in vain again. 'You can't run from me!' he cried, turning in circles now. 'Come on, give yourself up!'

I watched him for a moment, then sighed long and hard. Part of me wished I was that stupid. It would make life so much simpler ... and also twice as dull. On the screen, having finished his routine, the man was walking away under the deluge. I knew I couldn't sing. Dogs who sang sounded dreadful. But the dancing entranced me.

I thought about what my mum had said about being myself. That afternoon, watching the matinee with Penny, I knew what I had to do to achieve just that.

I would learn to dance! That would surely earn me a place in someone's heart and home. In my mind, being clumsy was something I could overcome. No matter how impossible it seemed, I had a dream to chase. And unlike my brothers and sisters with their tail fixation, I wouldn't let it get away.

2

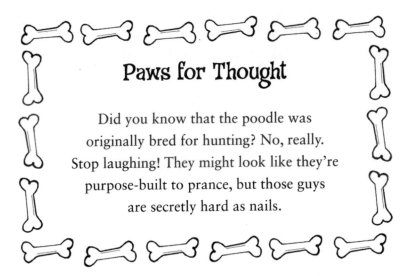

Paws for Thought

Did you know that the poodle was
originally bred for hunting? No, really.
Stop laughing! They might look like they're
purpose-built to prance, but those guys
are secretly hard as nails.

We were kept on the ground floor by a child gate at the foot of the stairs, which was fine by us. My brothers and sisters were happy playing their games in the kitchen and the front room, including a new one they'd invented called Upholstery Attack. Meanwhile, I lived in a dream world of dance. In my mind, I was a star.

In reality, whenever I closed my eyes and let my imagination carry me away, everyone just laughed.

'Here he goes again!' my brother once remarked as I swayed to and fro with that song playing in my mind. It made me happy, and I wagged my tail in time with the tune. I was only brought to a sudden halt when someone gave in to temptation and lunged for it.

'Hey, that's mine!' I complained from beneath a bundle of pups whose instincts had once again got the better of them. 'Calm down, all of you. Please!'

'But someone's got to chase that tail,' my big brother said as he hauled me from the heap. 'It's in the rules.'

'What rules?' I backed into a corner, folding my tail safely between my hind legs.

'Dog rules,' he said. 'You know? All food on the floor is fair game. The sofa is for sleeping on when Penny's back is turned. The postman is sad unless we bark at him every morning ... and tails fall off if we don't chase them.'

'They don't.' I looked at my brother, puzzled and amused. 'Do they?'

He showed me his tail.

'Well, do you want to risk it?'

I thought about this for a moment, and then dismissed it with a wave of my paw.

'The only rule in this house is that we're not allowed upstairs.'

Now it was my brother's turn to look baffled.

'What do you mean by upstairs?' he asked. 'Is it outside?'

'No, it's where the stairs take you,' I said, and gestured at the hallway.

He looked at me warily, as if I'd suddenly transformed into one of those weird hairless breeds with the bug eyes.

'Are you sure upstairs isn't outside? Because outside's out of bounds,' he said. 'Once we've left for our new homes and seen the vet for the last of our jabs, then we'll be set for the big wide world. Until then, there are bugs and viruses and worms out there that we could pick up on our paws. Any pup who steps outside is dicing with death.'

'Upstairs isn't outside,' I assured him. 'It's just a part of the house we're not supposed to explore.'

My brother turned to face the door.

'Upstairs sounds awesome,' he said, before turning to our brothers and sisters. 'Hey, fellas! Those steps behind the gate. Who knew they led somewhere? We should check it out.'

'We can't do that,' I hissed, urging him to be quiet in case Penny wondered what all the noise was about. 'It's not allowed.'

My older brother glanced at the others.

'What's the matter?' he asked, and faced back. 'Are you scared?'

'No,' I said quickly, aware that everyone was watching me. 'I'm not scared of anything.'

He nodded, as if I had told him quite enough.

'Glad to hear it,' he said eventually. 'A dog who wants to dance is one thing. We can make that our secret. But a fearful dog – a dog with no backbone – that won't go down well with anyone who's thinking of giving you a home.'

'I know that,' I said nervously. My brother was a sweet-natured soul, and he hadn't set out to make me feel uncomfortable on purpose. But I didn't like the attention I was getting from the other pups. Looking for a way out, I glanced around him and pretended to be surprised. 'Don't look now,' I said in a low voice, 'but I just saw your tail moving.'

'You did?' My brother raised his eyebrows. 'Seriously?'

I looked again.

'It's definitely back again,' I told him. 'Want me to get it for you?'

'No need,' he said, before twisting around so quickly that his hind legs left the ground. 'I've got it covered!'

Nobody mentioned the episode again, but I couldn't forget it. My brother had made out that I should be ashamed of my fascination with dance. That was fine by me. I could live with that. What bothered me was the thought that everyone had marked me down as a fearful dog.

For a pup who would soon be in need of a home, a label like that was bound to put people off. My brothers and sisters were naturally bouncy and inquisitive. I didn't want to be the one left trembling at the back. I had to prove I had guts. Not just to everyone else but to myself.

And there was only one way I could do it.

Whenever Penny went upstairs while my siblings were playing, she would be careful to shut the gate behind her. Sometimes when we were dozing in our basket with Mum she would close the kitchen door first. It made a creaking sound which often woke me up. Then I would hear activity on the steps, often followed by the front door opening and clicking shut again as Penny left the house. According to dog rules, anyone who went out for a walk without a four-legged friend at their side was considered weird. We talked about this at length amongst ourselves. Puppies were good fun but also very hard work, we decided. That would explain why Penny needed fresh air on her own twice a day.

For a long time after my big brother made his comments about my lack of courage, I kept a careful eye on her. I was looking for the opportunity to slip upstairs behind her, but she was always so quick to close that gate. My brothers and sisters showed no such interest. They were growing rowdier with every day that passed, which frankly left me with a headache. It also gave me an idea.

There was no guarantee that it would work, but I had no other option. Waiting until Penny had popped upstairs one afternoon, I put my plan into action.

'Hey guys!' I said, bounding into the front room where everyone was playing. 'There's something you need to know about the bookcase in the hallway.'

'Unless you've found a secret stash of treats, I doubt it'll be of interest to us,' my big brother said, scampering around the sofa. 'Mum says it's just a bunch of books about training dogs, but all of them are useless. Penny should give them to charity or something.'

I wasn't going to let his lack of interest stop me. Instead, I prepared to speak up so that everyone heard me.

'You're not going to believe this,' I told them all, and then waited until I had their full attention. 'It's got a tail.'

Sure enough, every pup in the room gasped in surprise, looking at one another as if this fact should've come to their attention ages ago. At once they rushed past me in a bid to reach the hallway. I followed calmly behind, and watched from the doorway as my brothers and sisters scrambled to find a way behind the bookcase so they could see for themselves. In the excited frenzy of barking and yelping, several actually tried to scale their way to the top. It came as no surprise to me whatsoever when the bookcase rocked forward and then toppled against the opposite wall. It wasn't very big or heavy, but nor was it designed to be a climbing wall. As books avalanched onto the floor, every pup dived for safety, and then shrank away from the staircase as Penny rushed back downstairs.

'What's all this?' she cried with some concern and quickly counted heads. 'Puppies, you must take more care of yourselves,' she added, and opened up the gate. 'Go and play in the kitchen while I clear this up.'

I didn't stop to watch her ease the bookcase back in position. I felt bad for being responsible for such a mess, but that's what little dogs do. At the same time, it had provided me with the opportunity I needed. In all the rush, Penny had forgotten to close the gate behind her. I glanced at my big brother, just to make sure that he was watching, and began to climb the stairs.

'You're going solo?' he asked, before Penny finally shooed all of them into the kitchen. 'That takes guts!'

It wasn't easy. Nothing ever is the first time you do it. Halfway up, I felt a little dizzy when I glanced back down. I told myself to keep going. Using my forelegs to grasp the step in front and my hind legs to push off from the one behind, I eventually grasped the landing carpet and hauled myself to the summit.

'Made it,' I whispered, panting at the same time. 'So, this is upstairs!'

I looked one way and then the other. To be honest, it didn't appear very different from downstairs. Just more rooms and nice pictures on the walls. Still, having got this far it was important for me to look around. I wanted to return to the other pups with a story of my courageous adventure that would surely earn their respect.

Then I heard a low chuckling. It was coming from a room whose door was ajar, and it sounded ever so slightly menacing. My first instinct was to flee. Then I reminded myself of the reason I was here. I took a deep breath and padded towards the room. I'm not sure what I was expecting, but when I peered around the door I couldn't help but gasp in surprise.

That was the moment I discovered that we weren't the only pets in the house. It was also when I learned that not all animals are as madcap and carefree as my brothers and sisters. As I peed in fear on the carpet – setting my house-training back a stage or two in the process – I realised that some could be very threatening indeed.

3

'Outside of a dog, a book is man's best friend.
Inside of a dog, it's too dark to read.'
Groucho Marx

ow, I'm sure you'll appreciate that lately I've been the one to leave an audience in awe. Back then, as I nosed my way into the room, it was me who stood there in astonishment.

'What are you doing here?' I asked.

The sun was streaming through an open window. On the carpet, two old Border collies were basking in the heat. They had shaggy coats with white ruffs and seemed equally surprised to see me. Both raised their heads when I appeared. I could tell from their scent that deep down they were friendly. It was the creature on top of the cupboard that caused my hackles to rise.

'Beat it, kid!' growled the ginger tom cat. 'Go back to Mummy. Upstairs is out of bounds. You could get hurt up here. Bad things might happen. Isn't that right, guys?'

The Border collies sniggered to themselves, which wasn't very polite.

'You want to do as Handsome Brad says,' said one. 'If you know what's good for you.'

'Handsome Brad doesn't get along with puppies,' the other one added, 'and you're a puppy.'

I sat at the doorway, intrigued by what I had found. The two dogs, a male and a female, both shot me pleading looks, but I didn't feel at all frightened. The cat called Handsome Brad glared at me. I simply smiled. After all,

Handsome Brad was a cat. It was against dog law to be scared of cats.

'Well, I'm pleased to meet you, Handsome,' I said.

The ginger tom looked a little pained at this.

'Just Brad will do,' he said, before glaring at the two collies below him. 'Why is this mutt still here?' he asked them. 'Obi, Indi, escort our friend back downstairs before I sharpen my claws.'

The dog called Indi looked at me anxiously.

'You really should go, kid,' she said.

'Brad's in charge around here,' added Obi. 'He's boss dog.'

I mouthed what he'd just said in case I'd heard it wrong. I looked back up at the cat, who narrowed his eyes at me.

'So, there's a cat who lives in this house who's boss dog? Wait until I tell the others!'

'Technically, Brad doesn't live here,' said Obi.

'He comes from a few doors down,' explained Indi, 'but there are more radiators in this house.'

'You know how it is for cats,' said Brad with a shrug. 'Our owners love us, even when they give us comedy names. They feed us and provide us with sofas to sleep on. They generally spoil us rotten. But hey, if there's a better offer ...'

'Dogs don't do that,' said Indi. 'We're loyal.'

'Yes, you are,' said Brad, focusing on me. 'You might say it makes up for the stupidity.'

'Penny doesn't know he enjoys the facilities,' Indi pointed out.

'I make my contribution,' insisted Brad, and swished his tail against the front of the wardrobe. 'Pest control.'

'Brad's good,' Obi assured me. 'There's no mice problem here.'

The ginger tom looked very pleased with himself.

'I'm guessing this is the first time you've come across a cold-blooded killer,' said Brad, looking as if he was about to pounce. 'How does it feel?'

For the first time, I felt as if perhaps I had strayed too far from my mum.

'I didn't mean to disturb you,' I told them. 'Mind you, if my brothers and sisters knew that a cat was in charge up here they'd have piled up to see for themselves.'

'OK, that's enough,' said Brad, sounding fed up all of a sudden. 'If the pup's too dumb to leave my personal space, let him come closer. I'll show him why I'm in charge around here.' With a flick, the ginger tom curled his tail. 'What do you think of that, huh? Come on. You can't resist it. You know you want to chase it.'

'Thanks all the same,' I said, 'but I'm not into chasing tails. It just doesn't interest me. Actually, all I want to do is dance.'

Brad's tail fell still. He twitched his whiskers and pushed his ears forward.

'Pardon me?'

Below him, Obi and Indi glanced at one another, and then looked back at me.

'Dance,' I said again, and rose onto four paws. 'One day I'm going to be a famous dancer.'

One of the dogs smirked, only to cower when Brad glared at him.

'If the puppy wants to dance, then let him show us what he can do,' said the cat. 'Come on, little fella. Dance for us.'

Unlike my brothers and sisters, these guys appeared to be showing an interest. I was flattered, and not a little nervous. Clearing my throat, I began to hum the song I had heard on the television. At the same time, I stepped forward with a jolly stroll. Both collies watched with interest as I jumped to one side and then the other, before trotting around them in a circle. I skipped and skittered as the song played in my head, gathering speed as well as confidence. There was little skill in what I was doing. It was all about passion. I just closed my eyes and turned in circles, which came to an abrupt halt when I smacked into the wardrobe.

I heard the cat screech. I just didn't realise that I'd knocked him from his perch until he fell on top of me.

'I'm so sorry,' I said, relieved at least that Brad had landed on his paws. 'That was an accident.'

'Yeah? Well so's this, then!' Without warning, the cat promptly threw himself at me. All at once, I found myself pinned to the floor. 'That was the dumbest dance act I have ever seen. Dumb and also dangerous.'

'I think Handsome Brad's pride has been wounded,' Obi said to Indi with a chuckle.

'Shut up!' the cat snarled. I was shocked by Brad's speed and also how close his claws were to my face. The rule about having no respect for cats, I decided, really needed to be rewritten. With a final glare, he jumped off me and raced back up to the top of the wardrobe. 'If it wasn't for the likes of you we'd still have the run of the house.'

'Penny prefers to keep us out of harm's way,' said Obi.

'Where we can get some peace and quiet,' Indi told me. 'At our age, puppies can be a bit of a pain.'

'What's your name, kid?' asked Brad, proceeding to lick one of his front paws.

I peered up at the cat, still rattled by his threats.

'I haven't got a permanent name yet,' I told him. 'None of us have. Our new owners will pick them when the time comes. Until then, we just have nicknames.'

'Let me guess,' said Brad, interrupting. 'You must be Twinkle Toes?'

Once the collies had stopped laughing, I drew breath to set them straight. At the same time, the sound of footsteps clattering up the stairs caused Brad's ears to twitch.

'OK, time to go,' he said, leaping in one graceful move to the window. 'You should do likewise. And then stay out of my sight. For your sake, you'd better hope you find a new home,' he added, preparing to leap for the sloping roof below. 'And fast!'

The footsteps had reached the landing. I wheeled around, fearing that Penny would surely make me pack my bags if she caught me. Both collies jumped up expectantly when the figure bounded into the room. It wasn't Penny, however, here to take them for a walk. It was her daughter home from school.

'There you are!' beamed Ashleigh, and dropped to her

knees to scoop me into her arms. 'I've found him, Mum!'
she called out. 'He's safe and sound.'

Ashleigh kissed me on the crown of my head. I glanced
at Obi and Indi, both of whom sighed and returned to
their spot in the sun.

'Nobody calls me Twinkle Toes,' I told them, trying
hard to sound tough despite being snuggled by a ten-year-
old girl. 'While I'm here, I only answer to the nickname
Ashleigh gave me.'

'What's that, then?' asked Indi.

Ashleigh rose to her feet just then, taking me with her.

'Pudsey,' I told them, before she whisked me from the
room. 'Just Pudsey.'

Paws for Thought

When people hit the big time, they often splash
out on a fancy car. Not me. I can't drive, after all.
Even so, I've indulged in a set of wheels. It's air-
conditioned, which is essential when we're in LA.
It's also Ashleigh-powered. Anyone who says
it's a customised pram can talk to the paw.

Ever since I've known her, Ashleigh has been dotty about dogs. While many of her friends were pony kind of people, girls who plastered their walls with gymkhana rosettes, Ashleigh filled her pinboard with photos of me, my brothers and sisters. She spent as much time as she could in our company. In short, if she wasn't at school she'd be playing with us. Going to bed was a bore because it meant time apart. I'd turn circles before settling, and then get up again to turn some more in the hope that Ashleigh would return. Eventually, I grew tired of nodding off feeling dizzy, and learned to assure myself that she would be there for us first thing in the morning.

It seems obvious to anyone who's got to know us recently, but right from the start I felt a close connection with Ashleigh. She had Penny's kind eyes, and long lashes that moved like butterfly wings when she blinked. Her smile could lift the lowest spirits, and she would do anything to help with our care and upbringing. She helped to wean us from our mum, brushed us morning and night, and kept our water fresh. Sometimes, when Penny reminded her that she had homework to do, Ashleigh would dutifully head upstairs, only to reappear with her school books and open them up on the floor beside us. My brother and sisters would help by piling onto the pages, because that was the surest way to get a tickle.

'She's a determined little thing,' Mum said. 'That girl is sure to go places.'

As for our future, the moment that I'd been fretting about for so long soon arrived. Two months after we came into the world, Penny started making plans to find homes for me, my brothers and sisters.

We all knew what was going on. We'd heard her on the telephone, talking to people who were interested in taking a puppy. As a result, we each went to extra lengths to behave like perfect dogs. All of a sudden, there were no accidents on the carpet, and the sofa remained out of bounds even when Penny's back was turned. My siblings continued to chase their tails, of course, but even they were beginning to grow out of that game. Once, I found my big brother looking out from the patio door. Several blackbirds were pulling worms out of the lawn. A squirrel eyed them from the fence, only to scuttle away when two wood pigeons settled in the branches of a nearby tree.

'There's just so much to chase out there,' he said dreamily. 'I can't wait.'

'It won't be long now,' I reminded him. 'Until then, there's always your tail.'

My brother glanced around as if he was being bothered by a fly.

'The trouble with tails,' he said, 'is that they're impossible to catch. It doesn't matter how hard I try, it always gets away. I reckon it's time to up my game.'

I sat beside him at the glass. For a moment, we watched the birds in silence.

'So, where do you hope you'll be going?' I asked him.

My brother glanced at me, which was a little bit like looking in the mirror.

'I want to be at the heart of a family,' he told me. 'We all do, right?'

As dogs, we looked identical. We were a unique breed, after all. Somehow, though, I'd inherited all the worry genes.

'I just hope a family wants me,' I told him.

'Don't fret,' my brother said reassuringly. 'You're the only pup who's managed to get upstairs. That took guts. You risked life and limb climbing that high. We were worried that the oxygen would be too thin to breathe!'

I chuckled and told him it was fine. As for my discovery of two collie dogs and a neighbour's cat, I kept that to myself. I hadn't come across Obi or Indi, or Handsome Brad, since that encounter. Nor did I intend to ever again. The collies looked as though they were nice dogs at heart, but that ginger tom clearly had a great deal of influence over them. Seeing as Brad hadn't taken kindly to me, I didn't want to make things worse for myself by encouraging my brother to seek him out.

'There really wasn't much up there,' I told him. 'I only had time to nose about for a minute or two before Ashleigh carried me down again.'

'Ah, sweet Ashleigh!' My brother tipped his head back and closed his eyes. 'I'll miss her when I'm gone.'

'Me too,' I said, thinking that where I was heading I'd probably have to settle for a battered shopping trolley as a companion. 'It won't be the same without her.'

'I expect she'll miss us, too,' my brother said, 'but I've heard Penny tell her we have to go.'

It was strange to hear my brother put our situation so bluntly. It made me sad to think that this house where we had grown up would soon be a thing of the past. Then both of us locked our attention on the blackbirds as they took off into the sky.

I remember the first family who came to visit us. They brought a whole lot of overexcitability with them, in the shape of three young daughters. Catching sight of them as they followed the path past the kitchen window, I had visions of being dressed up by them like a dolly, day in and day out (a vision that sends shivers down my spine to this day – I hate being dressed up with a passion). My brothers and sisters didn't seem at all concerned, racing to the front door to greet the visitors as soon as the bell rang. Penny and Ashleigh had to herd them back into the kitchen before opening the door. My mum looked on from her basket as my brothers and sisters swirled around them in the hope of being picked. I tried to join in, but it was such a scrum that I ended up being squashed against the dishwasher. Eventually, they chose my youngest sister. She was overjoyed, and though we were sad to see her go it was clear that she had found a loving home.

It was a pattern that was to be repeated throughout that week. Slowly, day by day, the number of puppies left behind grew smaller. Despite my best efforts, nobody picked me. As a result, I grew more fearful for my future, and that didn't help one bit. While my remaining siblings made every effort to draw attention to themselves, I just looked on anxiously. Even I knew that it wasn't an attractive look. Whenever people noticed me, they did so with pity in their eyes, and that just made things worse. Eventually, I found myself left with just one other pup.

My big brother was as surprised about this as me. He was the strongest and the rowdiest of the bunch, but for some reason that wasn't enough. 'Where have I gone wrong?' he fretted, pacing back and forth across the front room one afternoon. 'I don't understand it, Pudsey. I'm a good-looking crossbreed, aren't I? I'm fit and healthy. I'm not scared of men in uniform, or fireworks, or any of the things that are supposed to freak out a dog, and yet every time a family visits they walk away with someone else in their arms.

'What have I got to do to earn their attention?' he asked. 'Just don't say dance. Look how far it's got you.'

I have to admit I had tried out a few moves on the last family who visited. But I hadn't rehearsed anything, and no doubt it showed. All I had done was a little shimmy in front of the father, and his only response was to ask if perhaps I had fleas. It was humiliating, and once again resulted in me being left behind.

'Don't panic,' I told my brother. 'Mum says we just need to keep on being ourselves. She's convinced that's the best we can offer.'

My brother considered me for a moment.

'I've learned a new trick,' he told me, as if this was

some kind of confession. 'You're going to love it, and I hope the next family who visits will love it, too. All you've got to do is pretend to shoot me. Go on. Don't be shy. Give it all you've got!'

I looked at him long and hard, before raising my paw as he had asked.

'OK,' I said. 'Here we go. Get ready ... *bang*!'

At once, my older brother flipped onto his back and splayed his legs in the air. With his tongue lolling and his eyes glassed over, I thought for a moment that somehow I really had killed him.

'Hey,' I said, licking his face. 'Are you all right? Come on, this isn't funny!'

In response, my brother blinked, grinned and then sprang back onto his paws.

'What you've just witnessed, my friend, was a master-class in dog trickery! I think we can safely say that I'm the pup with all the talent.'

'It was good,' I agreed. 'You really had me fooled.'

'Yes, but was it cute enough?' My older brother came closer, a look of desperation in his expression. 'It's got to be cute, right? Cute is what finds us a family.'

Just then, Ashleigh floated into the front room. She beamed brightly on spotting us. Crouching down, she patted her knees and called us over. My brother and I raced to be first onto her lap.

As usual, I lost.

5

'Our dog chases people on a bike.
We've had to take it off him.'
Winston Churchill

That evening, a young couple visited with a toddler in tow. A little boy dressed in dungarees and a T-shirt with a shark embroidered on the front, he was friendly and playful, just like my brother and me. Having been handled by Ashleigh since the day we were born, we knew how to behave around children. In fact, as Penny saw it, our good nature meant we would be the ideal addition to a family with little ones. All we had to remember was that there could be no rough and tumble. That was fine by me, and even my big brother knew when to calm down. All those commands you teach us, such as 'sit', 'stay', 'heel' and 'please stop barking, you're driving me insane!'? It all sinks in eventually. We just had to be aware that it was usually the kids who didn't understand the rules.

This one was a little inquisitive, but he seemed fascinated by us. While his parents talked to Penny, who kept one eye on things, we both tried our hardest to bond with him. We were getting on really well when at one point he jabbed me in the ribs. I caught my breath and jumped away, startling the boy by my sudden movement. His cheeks turned red, and he looked as if he was about to cry. I was afraid that his parents would turn around and assume I had harmed him somehow. Fortunately, my brother stepped in.

'Don't worry, Pudsey,' he said. 'I'll handle this.'

Before the little lad had a chance to start wailing, he trotted up to him and turned side on. The boy looked at him in fascination, before prodding my big brother just as he had done to me.

'You got me!' my brother cried, and flipped over on his back. 'Goodbye, cruel world, it's been emotional!'

The boy looked dumbstruck. At the same time, his parents glanced around to see why my brother had just let out a yelp. Penny saw the pup upside down on the floor and smiled.

'This is his new trick,' she said. 'Watch.'

Taking this as his cue, my brother sprang back onto his feet. The boy squealed with delight, and wrapped his arms around him.

I felt a mix of emotions. It was kind of my brother to have distracted him, but in doing so he'd won the boy's heart. I smiled and looked at my front paws. As the couple declared that he was the dog of their dreams, I wondered how long it would be before Penny introduced me to the litter-strewn street corner of my despair.

There was nothing my mum could say to make me feel any better. Alone in the basket with her, I spent the next few days fretting.

'Penny would never dream of abandoning a dog,' she promised me. 'She'll find you the perfect home. Just you wait and see.'

'It's OK,' I told her, resigned to my fate. 'If I'm destined to wander through town and country for the rest of my life then so be it. Maybe I'll find friendship and adventure along the way, but I'll just keep on moving on.'

Mum eyed me suspiciously.

'Have you been watching television again?' she asked.

'Only an old dog show,' I confessed. 'But mostly the musicals. I'll miss those when I'm gone. Penny has good taste.'

'She does,' Mum agreed.

Every morning, I awoke assuming it would be my last day in the house. I didn't have a bag to pack, or even a knotted handkerchief for my belongings that I could tie to the end of a stick. If I'm honest, I didn't have any belongings at all. Still, I was prepared in my mind. I wasn't lonely. Ashleigh kept me company before and after school. I sat with her while she did her homework, not wishing to distract her, and at mealtimes I crouched underneath her chair. Every now and then, she would reward my loyalty by smuggling down a morsel from her plate. When she ate Alphabetti Spaghetti, I even learned to recognise some of the letters. I didn't think I had a book in me at the time, but given the chance I would've wolfed down more words per minute than any writer could rattle out across a page. I loved every minute, but it couldn't last. I was no longer a tiny scrap of a pup, and Ashleigh was growing older too. Her birthday loomed, in fact, and I wondered if I would still be around to see her blow out eleven candles on her cake.

At daybreak on her big day, my worst fears came true. I stirred in my basket to the sound of the kitchen door creaking open. Normally, I was wide awake and making lots of noise before Penny came downstairs (I'm more up with the bark than a night howl, if you know what I mean), but on this occasion she found me curled up in the basket. My mum was fast asleep, and didn't stir when I let out a whimper on seeing what Penny carried with her. The plain cardboard box could've been built for me. Sure enough, when she picked me up and placed me inside, there was only just enough room for me to turn around. I didn't fight to clamber out. There seemed no point. I just hoped that once she dropped me off she would leave the box behind. After all, I'd need some shelter on the street while I worked out my survival strategy.

'Bye, Mum, and thanks for everything!' I called out, and strained to hear her response. Nothing came, however, and I resigned myself to huddling in the corner.

I was prepared to be in that box for hours, even a day. I thought if Penny wanted to make sure I wouldn't find my way back, she'd take me somewhere far away. In the darkness inside that cramped space, time had no meaning. I just wondered what I'd find when we finally reached our destination, and where my next meal might come from. My thoughts were brought up short with a bump, however, when the box was set on the floor. We'd only been moving for about a minute, possibly much less than that, and all of a sudden I could see daylight through the cardboard flaps. I looked up, saw fingers easing the box open, and wondered what on earth was going on when a familiar face peered in.

'Pudsey!' cried Ashleigh, as tears welled in her eyes. 'Oh, Mum! He's all I ever wished for!'

We had come no further than the front room, and there was Ashleigh, all dressed up for her birthday. She looked totally shocked to see me – overwhelmed, even. For a moment, she rested her head on the side of the box. Then Grandma encouraged her to lift me out. I was still bemused when Ashleigh gathered me in her arms and hugged me tightly. Through my coat, I could feel her tears, but I knew they were tears of happiness. I looked at Penny, who was filming the moment on a video camera. She seemed set to blub as well.

'Happy birthday, Ashleigh,' she said with a smile, before turning to me. 'And welcome to your new home, Pudsey. You've just made someone the happiest little girl in the world.'

6

'Oh hai!'

I had found a home at last! Not only that, it was just where I wanted to be. I was as thrilled as Ashleigh, and also relieved. All my fears of being homeless just melted away. My mum must've known about Penny's plan when I raced back to tell her. She washed behind my ears one last time, and told me that from now on that was something I had to do for myself.

'You have responsibilities now,' she told me. 'Ashleigh is depending on you to be her faithful friend.'

It's a calling that every dog longs for. To be at someone's side for life is practically the reason for our existence. I took my duties very seriously, beginning by following every step she took around the house, and pining for her whenever she was at school, or back home and out of my sight for more than ten seconds at a time. If Ashleigh took a bath or a shower, I knew my place, which was slumped, apparently inconsolable, on the other side of the locked door. I was so happy with how everything had turned out. Even the two Border collies seemed pleased to see me. With my brothers and sisters gone, Penny removed the stair gate so that we could mingle freely. When Obi and Indi trotted down for the first time, they both welcomed me with a cautious but friendly round of bottom sniffing.

Of course, not everyone in the household was prepared to be so welcoming.

'Twinkle Toes?' Handsome Brad looked stunned when he came across me. He had slipped in through the back door while Penny was outside hanging the washing. I was lying on the kitchen tiles, practising my best hangdog look while waiting for Ashleigh to come home. The ginger tom took one look at me and his hackles rose. 'So, you're back …'

'I never left,' I told him, without lifting my head. 'I live here now. I'm Ashleigh's dog.'

Brad took a moment to digest this. Unless he'd just eaten something particularly manky from the bin, it looked as if my news had left an extremely nasty taste in his mouth.

'Then we have a problem,' he said, before padding across to our food bowls to see if there was anything left. 'You see, every pet in this house lives by my rules. It's how we get along. I'm afraid you can't just move in without my permission.'

'But I never moved out,' I said. 'I was born here.'

Brad looked around at me and glared.

'This house isn't big enough for us both,' he warned me. 'Don't make me kick you out.'

'Listen, Brad,' I said with a sigh, and raised my head from the floor. 'Can we start again? I really think we can be friends.'

'Friends?' he said, and headed for my basket. Mum was outside with Penny and the collies, which meant that Brad was free to curl up for a nap. 'You're a dog, and I'm a cat. We're hard-wired to hate each other. Our whole approach to life is fundamentally different. You chase things like a lunatic with your tongue slapping about all over the place; we use stealth and cunning. When your owner leaves the house you get shut in for your own safety; we're trusted to roam freely outside. Now, I think we both know what I'm saying here, but I'll spell it out because you're a dog. Yes, *a dog.* In my world that's code for stupid.'

'But you're friends with Obi and Indi,' I said, feeling a little bit hurt.

'No, I tolerate them,' said Brad as he settled down. 'They've overcome their stupidity enough to know when to stay out of my way.'

'Well, I'm happy to do the same,' I told him, and prepared to slink off to the front room. 'If you'll give me a chance.'

The cat made no reply, which I took to be a promising sign. I didn't want to fall out with Brad. I just wanted a quiet life. It wasn't easy, of course. Every time he showed up I'd feel obliged to make way for him.

On the upside, I wasn't to be confined to the house for much longer.

'It's a big day for you,' said Ashleigh one morning. 'You're allowed outside at last!'

We had visited the vet a few weeks earlier. With a clean bill of health and now that my second round of jabs had sunk in, I was safe to leave the house without dying within moments.

'Did you hear that?' Obi asked Indi, as they lounged together on their pillow beside the basket I shared with Mum. 'The boy is cleared to join us on walks!'

Indi's ears pricked up at the very mention of the word. A second later, my mum and both collies were crowding expectantly around Ashleigh, barking dementedly.

'Calm down everyone,' she chuckled. 'Pudsey's only fit for the garden at the moment. It's important not to over-exercise a puppy!'

'Carry him then!' said Obi, beginning to whine. 'Come on, Ashleigh. When a dog gets a promise of a walk, you can't back down.'

'She didn't mention a walk,' said my mum, and took herself back to the basket. 'You did.'

Obi glanced at Indi, who shook herself down in disap-pointment.

'The first rule of Walking Club,' she reminded him, 'is Never Talk About Walking Club. Not unless you know for certain a walk is going to happen. Otherwise we hear that word and automatically scramble for the door. It's a curse, I know, but that's how we manage it.'

With a sigh, Obi followed her back.

'How come the puppy gets all the fun?' he grumbled. 'Brad won't be happy.'

As the three dogs settled down once more, I followed Ashleigh to the back door. My heart was thudding with excitement. A pivotal moment in my life had arrived. At last, I would be free to roam and breathe fresh air.

'There's just one last thing to do,' she said, and reached for a bag on the side table. I watched her produce a fancy-looking collar, studded with plastic diamonds that sparkled in the light. It wasn't the manliest of collars, I admit, but when Ashleigh fastened it around me her face lit up with a smile. Finally, she fished from her pocket a silver tag that had my name and contact details engraved on it. 'In case you get lost,' she told me. 'Or dognapped!' I didn't like the sound of that one bit.

In a way, I was relieved that we were only starting out in the garden. Having spent weeks looking through the window, I didn't think there could be any surprises in store. Within moments of bounding out onto the lawn, I realised how wrong I was.

The noise was the first thing to stop me in my tracks. It was coming from the shed at the end of the garden. Joined to one side was a long wire run, which had been hidden from view from the house by some bushes. From inside I could hear a high-pitched shrieking and chattering. Whatever was causing the din, it sounded as if it was coming from more than one mouth.

With Ashleigh watching me from the gate, I crossed the garden cautiously, stopping at one point to satisfy an irresistible urge to scratch my hind paws furiously on the ground behind me. It wasn't until I peered around the bushes that I got a clear view. What I saw caused me to yelp and skitter back a step, knocking over a pot of geraniums in the process.

'False alarm!' chorused about six of what looked like

dozens of furry little creatures inside the run. They were each about the size of a shoe, with dishmop coats, little black eyes, long front teeth and whiskers. 'Sorry about that,' said the one closest to the corner as the others scuttled around. 'We hear the back door open and automatically assume it's feeding time.'

'Oh, I see,' I said, bemused by my discovery.

The creature offered me a long, studied look, which I half suspected was meant to be intimidating. But it was so fluffy – it looked as if it might even contain a battery compartment – that I just smiled back.

'You must be Twinkle Toes, right?' it asked me. 'We've heard about you.'

Cautiously, I came a little closer to the cage.

'My name is Pudsey,' I said. 'Clearly you've been speaking to Handsome Brad.'

'He drops by every now and then, just to see if Penny has left the door to the run open. Brad would pounce on us if he could, but that's never going to happen.' The creature paused and gestured over his shoulder at the others. 'Safety in numbers, you see?'

'What *are* you?' I asked.

'Guinea pigs,' it said. 'Penny breeds us for show.'

'There must be a lot of shows!' I joked. 'How many of you are there? Twenty? Thirty?'

The guinea pig fixed me with a hard stare.

'We are legion,' it said simply.

If I was taken aback by the creature's attitude, the sound of a ferocious hellhound tearing towards the other side of the garden fence prompted me to retreat by several steps. The guinea pig didn't blink, even when the dog tried and failed to jump into our garden.

'*Who is that?*' I asked, as the mutt could be heard slamming against the fence.

'Shredder,' said the guinea pig without turning. 'He has anger issues.'

'What breed is he?' I asked.

'A bulldog,' said the guinea pig, as if that should come as no surprise. 'Our presence upsets him for some reason. In fact, everything upsets him. You should hear him kick off when he catches sight of his own shadow.'

At the same time, another outbreak of squeaking emerged from the shed. A little ramp led up to an opening, from which appeared a female guinea pig that somehow looked more glamorous than the rest. Her coat was a beautiful blend of gold, black and white, as if she had been styled and colour-coordinated. There was something about it that made me think it had been in curlers overnight. As the guinea pig sashayed out into the sunshine, ignoring the sound of the frenzied bulldog, everyone cleared a path for her so that she could speak to me.

'Is this the dog that wants to dance?' she asked, in an abrupt voice that carried far.

'That's me!' I said proudly.

'Oh, really.' The guinea pig looked wistful for a moment. 'It's been a while.'

I had literally no idea what was going through her mind, but I thought it might be rude to press her about it. 'So, what's your name?' I asked instead.

'Smidgit,' she told me. 'You might know me from my modelling work. I featured on the cover of *Go Guinea Pigs!* – not once but three times. My finest years may be behind me, but back in the day I was hot stuff!'

'I'm sure,' I said, trying hard not to look amused. 'Maybe one day I'll know how it feels to be a success.'

Smidgit glanced at the girl still watching me from the gate.

'No doubt Ashleigh has plans for you,' she said, nodding as if she knew what was in store.

'The only thing I want to do is dance,' I told her.

Smidgit considered me for a moment. The bulldog continued to snarl and bay for blood on the other side of the fence, but the guinea pig's attention was locked on me.

'We can all dream,' she said, with just the slightest hint of pity in her voice, before turning and shuffling back to the shed.

7

Paws for Thought

You know how it is when you hit the teenage years?
You develop crushes at least twice a day (and on all
genders and species in my case), while your body
offers up new things to worry about such as volcanic
spots and odorous armpits. It's not that different for
dogs. We're naturally hairy from the moment we're
born, of course, and there's nothing wrong with being
smelly. In fact, the right sort of 'Eau de Chien' can be
a real pooch magnet. When I reached adolescence, at
around six months, I realised that going without
a bath was the key to finding love. Unfortunately,
Ashleigh disagreed, which probably explains why
I'm still single.

Whatever plans Ashleigh had for me, I wouldn't find out for a whole year. Apparently, I needed the time to grow big and strong. This wasn't difficult. With two bowls of food every day, and Walking Club commitments that took us from countryside to town and coast, I developed in both size and manner. My sense of balance and timing could've been better, but I made up for that by working with Ashleigh on obeying basic commands. As the months passed, I learned to sit, lie down, roll over and return to her side when she called me. I also learned to get along just fine with the guinea pigs and the other dogs.

When it came to dealing with Handsome Brad, the pack leader, I just kept out of his way.

Being a dog, it felt a bit humiliating having to steer clear of the cat each time he slipped into the house. But I worried about the consequences if I dared to break his rules. Brad had a ragged left ear which he claimed he'd picked up in a back-street brawl. He was also quick to stress that the other cat had come off worse, and that he wouldn't hesitate to issue the same kind of punishment to a dog if we dared to step out of line.

'I have nine lives, Twinkle Toes,' he once growled at me, when I was slow to shift from a spot by the radiator, 'and dogs have only one. So, who do you think's going to come out on top in a fight?'

Despite living in Brad's shadow, I quickly found myself right at home with Ashleigh. I especially looked forward to those moments when she chose to play music in her room. I would sway and circle, but she never once realised what was going on in my head. Instead, she would think I was restless and take me out for an extra walk.

Sometimes, I wondered what Ashleigh did have in mind for me. I half thought she intended to train me to be some kind of rescue dog. I wasn't sure if I was cut out to be a hero. I lacked the chiselled features of a dobermann, ridge-back or Great Dane, and after accidentally running into a whole carton of brandy butter in one of Penny's shopping bags that first Christmas I knew for a fact that alcohol disagreed with me. Even so, as long as it didn't keep me away from dancing then I planned to take on whatever challenge she had in store. If it made Ashleigh happy, nothing else really mattered.

Then came a day I'll never forget. The moment I learned what was expected of me, I freaked out completely.

Ashleigh had just turned twelve, and her grandmother was visiting. She had a birthday outing planned for her granddaughter, which was the cause of much excitement. Ashleigh adored Grandma, a little old lady who was prone to giggling all the time, and could be both gentle and generous. Whenever she popped round, her cardigan pocket was filled with treats. I wasn't the only dog who waited for that hand to dip into her pocket, of course, but this time she singled me out.

'Are you ready for an adventure?' she asked me, having

fed me a bit of broken biscuit from her palm. 'It's time we put you to the test!'

Five minutes later, Ashleigh and I were squeezed into the back of Grandma's hatchback. I had no idea where we were heading, but I soon had a hunch that it might take a while to get there. I'm not saying Grandma was a slow driver. I'm sure she had our safety uppermost in her mind, but I did wonder whether we should've just walked as another family meandered past us on their bicycles.

'This is it,' Ashleigh said to me, as we unfolded ourselves from the car.

'It's my treat,' Grandma said. 'A present for you and Pudsey!'

I looked around. Across the courtyard was an imposing building with high windows and big barn doors. One of the doors was open. It was too gloomy inside to make out very much, but I could see sand on the floor and what looked like a red and white striped gate of some description. Just then there was an almighty whoosh of air as something hurtled over the gate, accompanied by fierce instructions from someone who sounded like a drill sergeant. Warily, I glanced up at Ashleigh as she clipped the leash onto my collar. Was this some kind of army training camp? I thought to myself. If she planned to school me in explosives detection, then she could expect to see me climb straight back inside the car and lock all the doors with my paw.

'Don't be shy,' said Grandma, leading the way to the building. 'This is supposed to be fun!'

Inside the barn, it took a moment for my eyes to adjust to the change in light. When everything came into focus, I realised that the blur I had seen outside was in fact another dog.

A superhuman one, I thought, judging by what it was doing.

The dog, a white German shepherd, was charging around a vast obstacle course. From seesaws to tunnels, tyre jumps to raised walkways, it negotiated everything at top speed and with no apparent fear or hesitation.

'What do you think?' Ashleigh asked me. 'Exciting, isn't it?'

Exciting wasn't the word I would've used to describe the scene. Absolutely hair-raisingly terrifying was a closer description. Following further instructions from a stern-looking woman in the middle of the barn, the German shepherd sped up a steep ramp before effort-lessly trotting across a narrow beam. I didn't like the look of it one bit. As soon as the dog raced down the other side, it snapped around then sat obediently beside the woman. She looked moderately satisfied with its per-formance. Personally, I was surprised that the dog wasn't wearing an eye mask and a cape, or at least some army fatigues.

'Welcome to the agility training centre, Pudsey,' said Grandma. 'You're next.'

'What?' I looked across at her, unsure if she was joking.

Ashleigh patted me reassuringly.

'I've always wanted to do this. Canine agility is totally

safe. Dogs love it, too! I know you're up to the challenge.'

I felt my heart rising into my mouth. All of a sudden, training to sniff out explosives sounded like a much safer option than this. I peered around at the course once more. Most of it seemed to take place about six feet off the ground. Bearing in mind that I'm knee-high to Ashleigh on a good day, it was daunting to say the least. The woman with the shepherd came across to speak to us. She was wearing a sweatshirt with the name of the centre across it. I figured she must be in charge. As she instructed Ashleigh on the best way to tackle each obstacle, the shepherd took one look at me and said:

'It's your first time, isn't it?'

The dog had a deep voice and sounded cool and confident. I wondered whether he was in training to be an international spy or something.

'How can you tell?' I asked.

He glanced at my legs. All four of my knees were knocking.

'A word of advice,' he said as we sniffed and circled each other. 'Don't look down. It's bound to freak out nervous dogs like you. But there's really no cause for concern. Just listen to the commands, keep your breathing under control, and you should get round without an emergency call-out from the vet.'

I peered at the course once more.

'So, why are you here?' I asked him.

'If I told you,' said the shepherd, 'I'd have to kill you.'

I took a breath, but couldn't follow it up with another

one because at that moment the woman wished Ashleigh good luck and stood back with the dog.

'Go for it, Pudsey!' said Grandma, and settled in a plastic chair to watch. 'Break a leg!'

Ashleigh led me to a low table with a marker beside it labelled with a '1'. Peering around, I realised each obstacle had a numbered marker. There were twenty in total, which formed a route around the course from start to finish. I didn't think I'd make it into double figures without passing out.

'You can do this,' Ashleigh assured me. 'I believe in you!'

We had spent a year bonding together. I couldn't just walk away. Grandma had arranged this as a special day in Ashleigh's life. Who was I to spoil it for her?

'OK,' I said to myself, and puffed out my chest. 'Let's go to work!'

The obstacle course, in my opinion, was designed to bring a dog as close to disaster as humanly possible. As soon as I left the table, with Ashleigh jogging along beside me, and approached the first hurdle, my life flashed before my eyes. I couldn't say why, but the thought of climbing a ramp and crossing a plank filled me with dread. Carefully, I placed one paw in front of the other. Each step up the ramp caused me to feel dizzy and sick, but it wasn't until I reached the top that I realised what the problem was.

I was scared of heights. Not just scared but petrified.

I remembered the advice that the white German shepherd had given about not looking down, and promptly felt compelled to ignore it. I was no more than a couple of feet off the ground, but just then it felt like sixty flights of a skyscraper. I had to see for myself.

'Ohmygodohmygod … oh my god I'm going to faint I'm going to faint, I'm going to faint!!' I yelped, seeing Ashleigh. 'Save me!'

Concerned by the noise I was making, she reached up and touched my front paw.

'You're doing just great, Pudsey,' she reassured me. 'There's no going back now.'

There was an awful lot of going back I could've done if I'd been with anyone else but Ashleigh. I didn't care that the shepherd and the instructor were watching me. When I glanced across at them, both were staring at the sand, as if they couldn't bring themselves to watch any more. I glanced back at Ashleigh. She mouthed some words of encouragement. Despite feeling frozen to the spot, I looked into her eyes and knew that I had to see this through.

'Be strong,' I told myself, and focused on the way ahead once more. 'What are you? A dog or a mouse?'

With Ashleigh's hopes upon me, I set out on the crossing. It felt like I was walking a tightrope not a plank, but I got there in the end. And once I did, Ashleigh promptly raced to the next obstacle, urging me towards it.

'Come on, Pudsey. Through the tunnel!'

This, I thought, should be easier. Daintily, I made my way down the ramp and plunged into the tube.

It was then I discovered that I wasn't just scared of heights. I was scared of the dark as well.

'Ashleigh?' I called out quietly, having found myself consumed by darkness. 'Ashleigh, I can't see anything. I'm frightened, Ashleigh. I think there's something in here with me. Something big and bad. No wait! That's my tail.'

Just as I was about to plunge into a full-blown panic attack, a chink of light appeared up ahead.

'This way, Pudsey,' she said, holding open the canvas flap so that I could see where I was going. 'You're doing brilliantly!'

As I crept towards the light, whining all the way, I wondered what I'd have to do to be judged appalling. I knew full well that my performance left a lot to be desired, but that didn't stop Ashleigh from pushing onwards. Honestly, it was like some dreadful SAS initiation ceremony, repeated from one obstacle to the next. Even the seesaw had me rattled. It should've been simple, but when it tipped as I passed over the centre I felt as if I was plunging through thin air. By the time my paws reached the ground, having leapt the final gate, I was in a complete state. Not that I let Ashleigh know.

'Good boy!' She wrapped her arms around me, hugging me tight while Grandma clapped heartily. 'I knew you'd be a natural!'

Had Ashleigh looked in my eyes just then, she would've been reminded of the kind of glazed stare you get from someone who has just climbed off a rollercoaster for the first and last time in their life. Instead, I kept my gaze from hers and told myself that at least it was over. Ashleigh's special day was done and she looked very happy. I hoped that now we would move on to something less traumatic.

'You both did very well,' said Grandma, when Ashleigh picked me up and joined her. 'But you'll need to practise hard if you want to enter Pudsey into competition.'

8

Dog agility – who's the Daddy now?

So, Ashleigh had a dream. I wanted to share it, I did. But frankly, it was more like a nightmare for me. Even so, once I knew how important it was to her, I swore to myself that I would overcome my fears. What's more, I wanted to make her proud of me while I was at it.

I've got to be honest. In the beginning, it was tough. The odds of success were stacked against me. In an attempt to overcome my phobias, I followed the collies' advice. This came about after Indi told me how she had helped Obi overcome his unusual fear of water.

'How?' I asked, keen to try anything. 'If I could learn to be comfortable with heights and dark spaces, life would be a whole lot easier for me.'

'It's all about gently introducing a dog to the thing it most fears,' said Indi. 'Over time, the more familiar the dog becomes with it, the less frightening it seems.'

I settled before their pillow, keen to find out more.

'So, what did you do to help Obi?' I asked her.

'Oh, nothing much,' she said a little awkwardly.

Meanwhile Obi was beginning to scowl at the memory.

'Let me tell you,' he continued. 'We were walking beside the canal one day. Penny had let us off the leash, and Indi was carrying the tennis ball in her mouth.'

'I like to carry the ball,' said Indi. 'It's a comfort thing.'

'Except for that day,' said Obi bitterly. 'Do you know what she did with it, Pudsey? Even though she knew water terrified me, she dropped it into the canal.'

'So?' I glanced from one collie to the other.

'So, I'm a dog!' declared Obi. 'I can't ignore a loose ball. All of a sudden, it represents the very purpose of my existence. Nothing else matters but retrieving it!'

'Even if it's in the canal,' Indi pointed out. 'It was my way of gradually introducing Obi to the thing he feared the most.'

'Maybe we should discuss the definition of gradual,' said Obi, facing his companion. 'There was nothing gradual about it. One moment I was on the canal path, the next I was swimming with shopping bags. In fact, I shudder to think what else was in there,' he went on, sounding increasingly emotional at the memory. 'Everyone knows canals contain body parts!'

'But did it work?' I asked. 'Did it beat your phobia?'

'Oh, sure,' said Obi. 'Back home, Penny had to hose me down three times because I stank so badly. By the end of that day I was intimately familiar with water.'

I thought about this for a moment.

'Do you think the same approach could work for me?' I asked. 'Now I know I'm scared of darkness and heights, I really want to beat it.'

'That depends,' said Indi. 'Are you up for the challenge?'

'You bet I am!' I told her. 'Ashleigh's dream depends on it.'

I genuinely believed that the collies had my best intentions at heart. It was only when they put their plan into practice that I questioned if they were the right dogs to help me.

'I appreciate the effort you've made,' I called out, breaking the silence after a matter of minutes, 'but I'm not sure about this.'

It was a school day. Penny was out, leaving just us dogs inside. As soon as we found ourselves alone, Indi and Obi had prepared the front room by not entirely successfully dragging the curtains together. They then pushed a chair in from the kitchen, as if herding a stray sheep, before instructing me to hop onto it. As a result, I found myself on my own in the half-light wondering how long this would take.

'Is it working?' asked Obi from behind the door. They had been careful not to shut it completely, to stop me from being trapped. So I was sitting, on a chair, in a slightly dim room with the door ajar.

'Let's just say I'm not quite at the limit of my endurance,' I told him.

'That's good,' replied Indi, who was in the hallway as well. 'We need to introduce you to your fears gradually.'

'The thing is …' I said, trying to work out how to break the news to them gently. 'I'm not frightened in here at all.'

'Fabulous!!' Indi barged the door open. 'Then you must be cured!'

Before I could make things a bit clearer to them, both collies rushed in and circled the chair I was standing on.

'We knew it would work,' said Obi with a bark. 'Nothing can hold you back now!'

'Let's hope so,' I said. 'Except maybe the dark. And heights.'

But neither Obi nor Indi were listening. I appreciated their enthusiasm, but as I hopped off the chair, I realised that my fears were something I would just have to face on my own.

My mum appeared at the door just then, drawn by all the fuss. She could tell simply by looking at me that I was still worried about the challenge I faced.

'What you need is a special place in your imagination,' she told me. 'Your fears can't touch you there.'

I took Mum's words of advice with me to the next training session with Ashleigh. As soon as my heart began to race, first on the raised plank and then inside the tunnel, I closed my eyes and tried to picture myself somewhere else.

There was just one problem with this, I discovered. I didn't have a special place.

No matter what I conjured up in my mind, nothing worked for me. I went from my basket to the front room and even to a spot in front of the guinea pigs' run that got a lot of sunshine. I loved each of those places, but in the middle of an obstacle course, none of them made me feel any better. All I could do was grit my teeth and hope I would make it to the finish line.

We repeated the process several times a week, and I realised very quickly that Ashleigh was as passionate about agility as she was about me. Together, we'd spend hours practising on the course. When summer came, we went out into a field with some equipment and worked out there. Eventually, in my opinion, I went from hopeless to passable and then finally pretty good. At the same time, I grew less frightened of heights and dark tunnels. Both still made my hackles rise, but steadily I grew more familiar with them as we trained. After a few months, even the white German shepherd congratulated me on how far I'd come.

'Nice job, Pudsey,' he said, as we left after another long session one evening. 'Great timing and coordination.'

'Really?' I stopped in my tracks, which brought Ashleigh to a halt as she was leading me out by a leash. To hear another dog compliment me on two skills I'd always felt I lacked came as quite a surprise. 'I hardly think I'm a natural.'

'I mean it,' he said. 'I see a lot of dogs come through here. You're starting to shine.'

I gestured at Ashleigh, who was waiting for me to stop sniffing the other dog.

'I'm doing it for her,' I told him. 'We're in competition soon. It's my first time.'

The shepherd nodded appreciatively.

'At the standard you're performing,' he said before we left, 'I doubt it'll be your last.'

The white German shepherd was right. I'm pleased to say that I didn't embarrass Ashleigh at our first event. In fact, we almost won! It wasn't long before our first competition victory arrived. From then on, with Penny and Grandma in tow, our weekends were taken up with show after show. Each time, we returned home with another rosette or medal, which Ashleigh displayed with pride. Mum, Obi and Indi were very impressed, as were Smidgit and the other guinea pigs.

The same could not be said for Handsome Brad.

'When it comes to agility,' he once said with a sneer, 'you just can't beat a cat. We don't need to train for hours on end. It's something of a gift.'

Brad addressed us from the roof of the guinea pigs' run. Indi, Obi and I were lying on the grass in the sun. Brad was in a bad mood, having been discovered in the kitchen by Penny and shooed out of the house. It happened quite a lot, but never stopped him from returning.

'Why don't we see many cat agility competitions then?' asked Obi, stretching and rolling onto her back.

'You would,' said Brad, and rose to prowl the length of the run. Beneath him, the guinea pigs looked up warily. 'But we cats consider that sort of thing rather, well ... pointless. I mean ... what's in it for you?'

'I get treats,' I told him defensively. 'And if I'm really good at the end then Ashleigh throws my red plastic chew for me.'

Brad said nothing. He just smiled to himself and settled at the end of the run.

'Pudsey's come a long way,' said Indi. 'We're very proud of him.'

The ginger tom stared at the collie until she apologised for speaking out of turn.

'So, what's next?' he asked me. 'Any more agility medals would just be showing off.'

'I'm not sure,' I said, with my head resting on my paws. 'I'm thrilled for Ashleigh. She's done an amazing job in training me, and I know that it's her dream come true. But even though I enjoy seeing her have such a good time, it all just leaves me feeling a little ... flat.'

Handsome Brad watched my torso heave with a sigh.

'Still dreaming of dancing, Twinkle Toes? Wake up and smell the kibbles, buddy. You're a dog!'

'Pudsey is not just a dog.' Everyone turned to the shed, just as Smidgit glided out onto the ramp. The shed served as the guinea pigs' sleeping quarters, but Smidgit, the eldest and most glamorous of them all, treated it more like a dressing room. As she scuttled down the ramp, her lustrous coat bounced and waved as if she'd just had it blow dried. 'He's overcome many obstacles to get where he is today,' she went on, seemingly unconcerned by the tom cat overhead. 'Before he started agility, we all knew Pudsey as an awkward, gangly mutt who was scared of everything. You remember what he was like?' she finished. 'Basically he was an embarrassment.'

'Steady on,' I said in protest, but Smidgit didn't appear to hear me. Instead, she twirled around as if pacing a stage.

'Pudsey, my dear, if you have a dream,' she said, 'then you owe it to yourself to chase it.'

'Chase?' Obi's ears pricked up at the word. 'What? Where?'

'You see,' said Smidgit. 'A dog never gives up on a chase.'

Indi turned to me.

'It's true,' she said. 'Every now and then when I catch a glimpse of my tail, I think about going for it, just for old times' sake.'

I glanced at Handsome Brad. He shook his head before cleaning his whiskers.

'You're wasting your time,' he said. 'Whoever heard of a dancing dog?'

I felt confused by what I was hearing. I wanted to act on Smidgit's advice, but Brad's warning rang horribly true. I rose to my paws, stretched forwards and then backwards.

'I'm going for a lie down in my basket,' I told everyone. 'I need to think.'

'Don't hurry back,' said Handsome Brad, and he hopped off the guinea pig run to take my place in the sun.

9

Paws for Thought

I trained in agility for five-and-a-half years.
That's a long time in a dog's life. In human terms,
it's the equivalent of fifteen years ... no, wait, I've
got that wrong. Nineteen ... hang on. One dog
year is the equivalent of seven in your world,
which adds up to what? Twentysomething?
Oh, I don't know. I'm only good
with musical numbers.

Eventually, I decided that Smidgit was right. If I ignored my dream, one day I would look back on my life with regret. It left me with a renewed sense of hope, and with respect for the under-appreciated wisdom of guinea pigs.

I also wanted to prove to Handsome Brad that he was wrong.

It helped that the family enjoyed music. Penny often had the radio switched on in the kitchen, and Ashleigh would always do her homework with songs filling her ears. It gave me plenty of opportunity to flex my limbs and get into the rhythm. I should say that I was also taken out on a lot of extra walks during this time as a result of my constant wiggling. I couldn't expect Ashleigh to recognise that I was learning how to dance. Through her eyes, it was understandable that she'd assume that I was restless and reach for my leash.

'I don't know what's got into him lately,' she told Penny one afternoon. 'Every time I sit down to do my homework, Pudsey starts clowning around behind me.'

Penny gave me a long look.

'He does it in here sometimes, too,' she said. 'Maybe it's a phase he's going through.'

It wasn't a phase. Dancing was in my genes. I know they would never have said anything to hurt me, but I felt sad to think that my efforts to get into the beat looked so comical to them. It knocked my confidence each time they mentioned it, until eventually I felt too embarrassed to dance in their presence. As a result, even though my heart urged me to keep going, my paws refused to keep on tapping. Instead of climbing out of my basket whenever Penny turned up the volume for a favourite tune, I just sighed and rested with my head on my paws.

My downcast spirits hadn't gone unnoticed by the other animals in the house, though. When my back was turned, usually while I mooched and dozed and mooched again, they hatched a plan to get me back on track.

It was the dogs who put it into practice one weekday afternoon. We were alone in the house with the radio, which Penny always left on to keep us company. I remember it was the midweek chart rundown. I wasn't really paying much attention to it – unlike my mum, which was a first.

'I love this week's number four,' she said. 'It's coming up after this next tune.'

I glanced across at her. She was already looking at me.

'Since when did you like chart music?' I asked.

'This song's special,' she said. 'I can't help tapping a paw to it.'

I lifted my head, intrigued.

'What's it called?' I asked.

'All I know is that it's catchy,' she said. 'Trust me, you'll like it.'

I continued to eye my mum, unsure if she was playing with me. She looked totally serious, however.

'Well, I'll listen out for it,' I told her. 'From right here in my basket.'

As far as I was concerned, with Ashleigh at school, this was an opportunity for a good kip. I settled back and closed my eyes.

The next time I opened them, it was to the opening bar of the song my mum had been looking forward to. It was a big groove-driven number but I didn't stir because of the song. No, I woke to an almighty racket as the kitchen door crashed open and two insane collies pranced their way in.

'Good grief!' I said, sitting upright. 'What are you doing?'

Obi and Indi responded by each turning full circle in opposing directions. They then repeated the move the other way round, before high fiving each other with their front paws.

'We're getting the funk on, baby!' said Indi, strutting backwards at the same time.

'Join us,' added Obi, and bobbed his head. 'Come and show us how it's done!'

Slowly, I realised what was going on. I shook my head, smiling at the same time.

'Don't be shy!' said Obi, raising his voice to be heard over the radio. 'Let's tear up the dance floor!'

'Come on, Pudsey!' Indi chimed in. 'It's time to let the dogs out!'

'OK, OK!' I climbed out of my basket. 'You got me.'

For the next few minutes, once I'd got up to speed, I joined the collies in a boisterous workout. Indi and Obi gave me centre stage, and I really let myself go. We probably just looked like a bunch of horse-playing dogs, who'd scoffed down a party pack of Haribo, but that didn't matter to us. We covered every tile of the kitchen floor with an energy that left us panting. When the tune came to an end, Mum barked appreciatively.

'You mustn't give up dancing, Pudsey! It brings out the best in you.'

I took a second to catch my breath, while the collies headed for the water bowl.

'That was fun,' I told her after a moment, 'but there's no future in it for me.'

'Oh, Pudsey!' she said, crestfallen.

But my mind was made up. 'In my head I can dance. It's just when I do it for real ... as you saw for yourself, I'm just another overexcited dog in need of a walk.'

'It's all about practice,' said Obi, raising his head from the bowl. 'You worked hard at agility, and look how far that's got you.'

'You just have to do the same thing again,' said Indi. 'Only this time we're here to support you.'

'We all are,' Mum added. 'Even the guinea pigs have volunteered to help you train.'

'Really?' I looked around at the three dogs. 'You'd all do that for me?'

'Hey,' said Obi, and circled on the spot. 'Who doesn't like dancing?'

My friends were true to their word. Whenever Ashleigh was at school and Penny had popped out, I could practise under the watchful eye of a trio of pooches who had taken my dream to their hearts. We had a wild time for weeks on end, but to be honest I'm not sure how much my dancing improved. The collies just liked to shake their thing, while my mum's critical eye went no further than making sure I didn't slouch and saying that I looked lovely. Still, I was so grateful for the effort they made, and happy to have a good time with them.

The guinea pigs, however, pursued a different approach. With no music available down by their run, Smidgit improvised with the help of her friends. She also did so with a sense of discipline.

'Are you ready, Pudsey?' she asked me once. 'Remember to keep good time. So long as you stick to my beat, you can't go wrong.'

I was facing the cage, as instructed. In front of me, the guinea pigs had arranged themselves side by side, from one end to the other, with Smidgit in the middle. It had come as news to me that they were seasoned line dancers. Masked from the house by the hedge, I realised they had plenty of privacy to teach themselves all manner of hobbies, interests and pursuits. It was Smidgit who kept them in sequence, stamping her paws and calling out directions. None of them seemed distracted even by Shredder, the bulldog in the garden behind us. As he repeatedly head-butted the fence, they didn't even blink.

'Ready when you are,' I told Smidgit, and prepared to follow her moves.

'And, two, three, four, here we go. Right paw behind left paw, that's it. Step left to left side, right paw to right side, and repeat …'

Smidgit could be fierce, but also encouraging. She was a demanding but skilful choreographer, and slowly my self-confidence returned. Sometimes, the other dogs joined in. It made things more challenging, especially as Obi had a tendency to go in the opposite direction to everyone else, but every now and then we'd make it through to the end without a hitch. The last time we finished a near faultless routine, however, my happiness didn't last long.

'Look at you all,' said Handsome Brad as he appeared on the roof of the shed. 'This is a joke, right?'

'Well, nobody's laughing here.' Smidgit looked up and scowled. Unlike us, she wasn't scared of the ginger tom, probably because he couldn't lay a paw on her. 'Pudsey has been practising hard.'

'So I see.' Brad made himself comfortable on the felt roof. 'Clearly practice doesn't make perfect.'

'Oh, leave him alone,' she said, as the other dogs tried hard not to catch Brad's eye.

'Hey, trust me,' the cat said. 'I care about him as much as you guys. I'm just concerned that he's shaping up to look like a big fat fool. I mean, really, Pudsey. You need to take a long look at yourself.'

'His dancing is improving all the time,' said Smidgit, but Brad was no longer listening to her.

'Do this one thing for me.' Effortlessly, the cat jumped down onto the cage and then the grass. 'Come inside the house for a minute with me. There's something I want you to see.'

Brad set off before I could reply. I glanced around at the dogs and the guinea pigs, and then turned to follow Brad when he called my name once more.

When we reached the kitchen, Penny was unloading the dishwasher. Without a sound, or an apparent care, the ginger tom padded in behind her. I did my best to follow in kind, but Penny noticed me.

'Where are you off to?' she asked.

I looked for the cat but he was gone. Brad would only blame me if I alerted her to his presence, so I spent a moment being petted before hurrying into the hall to find him.

'I don't have all day,' he said, from the foot of the steps, and then bounded to the top.

Upstairs, Brad directed me into Ashleigh's bedroom. She was at school at the time, but the clock radio was still playing at a low volume.

'What now?' I asked, turning to the cat.

'What now is you dance,' he said. 'Go ahead. The light's particularly revealing in here.'

My first instinct was to walk out. Handsome Brad had led me up here simply to humiliate me. Then I wondered whether this was the moment when I could shut him up for good.

'Very well,' I said. 'You'd better watch from Ashleigh's desk. I'll be making full use of the space.'

Brad looked amused, but did as I had asked.

A ballad was playing on the radio. It was an uplifting tune and I began by swaying in time.

'Very good,' said Brad, with a hint of sarcasm in his voice. 'Nice timing.'

At the punchy chorus, I broke out my best move. It began by clapping my front paws together followed by a back kick. Brad began to nod and whoop.

'You see,' I said breathlessly. 'I *can* dance!'

Brad responded by making a circling gesture with his paw.

'Now turn around.'

'No problem!'

I snapped around to show how quickly I could move, and that's when I found myself facing Ashleigh's mirror.

'Don't stop,' he said, after I had paused for a moment. 'Let the music move you, man. Show me what you do.'

Taking a breath, I continued to bob and shuffle. This time, however, I did so with my eyes locked on my own reflection. My expression looked pained, and more so when I saw how my backside rose and fell behind me. Frankly, I looked like I was about to heave my breakfast all over the carpet. I struggled on for a matter of seconds, rocking backwards and forwards. Then Handsome Brad started laughing. As the music faded, my shoulders sagged and I let my head simply hang.

'I can't dance,' I said to myself. 'Who am I kidding?'

Brad took a while longer to regain his composure.

'You see!' he said, and jumped down beside me. 'It's a joke! One big giggle, Pudsey, and all at your expense. You can chase your dream all you like, but it'll get you nowhere. Give it up. Move on.'

I glanced at Handsome Brad. He burst into another fit of laughter. Just then the DJ started talking. I hoped he would never play another song again.

'I need some time alone,' I said, and slunk out of the room.

10

'A dog has the soul of a philosopher.'
Plato

P enny didn't notice me drift back through the kitchen. Had she done so she would've stopped me and questioned why I looked so thoroughly crushed. Instead, while she sat at the table with a cup of tea and the newspaper, I sloped into the yard for some fresh air.

Outside, I was surprised that I could still hear Handsome Brad chuckling to himself so clearly. Feeling haunted by him all of a sudden, I peered up and saw him sitting on the ledge outside Ashleigh's bedroom window. He was looking out towards the late sun, basking in what was left of the heat. I couldn't bear to hear him any more. Nor could I face my friends at the bottom of the garden. I had to get away. I needed to be alone with my thoughts.

The front gate was easy to open. I had seen Ashleigh and Penny do it many times before. I simply positioned my nose underneath the latch before levering it upwards and then pushing my way onto the pavement. I didn't think about where I was heading, I just hit the road and started walking. All I carried with me were the broken remains of my dreams. I wanted to shake loose from my thoughts all my hopes of being a dancer. I was determined to leave all that behind for good, but no matter how far I roamed they stayed with me. Lost in thought, I crossed junctions without looking, and ignored the friendly but concerned glances of some of the people I passed.

As the light gradually faded from the day, however, I began to attract attention of a more uncomfortable kind. I'd reached a run-down part of town. A lot of the shops were boarded up, and it had been some time since the street's gutters had seen a sweeper. Outside a betting shop, tied to a post by a length of string, a Rat terrier stared at me as if I didn't belong. Still, I didn't really care. I had never felt so empty inside myself.

I'd always believed that I was born to dance. What a waste of time that had been.

By the time the moon sailed into the sky, and the street lights flickered on, I started to feel hungry. I had no idea of the time. I'm a dog, after all, but my belly told me it had been a long while since breakfast. It wasn't just my stomach that felt empty, but also my heart. I had roamed far from home, I realised. Across the street, in a little mews lined with potted plants, an elegant-looking lady out walking two chihuahuas had stopped outside a front door. She was searching in her handbag for something. I watched the tiny dogs waiting patiently at her feet, turning circles with excitement when she eventually found the keys. She unlocked the front door and they scuttled in, practically pulling her over the threshold. Then she closed the door, evidently home at the end of the day, and it left me feeling utterly alone.

'Oh, Pudsey,' I said to myself. 'What have you done?'

Just then I knew what I was missing. Walking away from my dream of being a dancer was one thing, but in doing so I had also turned my back on my family. I looked around. The street stretched away for miles in both directions. I had turned so many corners that I could be certain of just one thing. I had lost my way.

With a sigh, I trudged on. I figured if I kept going I might come across a route from Walking Club. Instead of heading onwards with my eyes on the pavement, my attention turned to the houses and flats, their lights on and their curtains closed. I imagined all the people and their pets tucked up inside. It was growing cold, and there was a sound of distant thunder that I didn't like one bit. Overhead, inky clouds were beginning to claw across the evening sky. I steered a wide path around a group of youths in hoodies. A couple of them noticed me, exchanged some muttered words and laughed. I didn't fit in around here. I knew that. Handsome Brad once said that my face resembled a stuffed toy that belonged at the foot of a child's bed. It hadn't bothered me at the time, but on the wrong side of town after dark, I wished I looked a little more street tough.

'Hey, pretty boy!' a voice called out at one point, causing my hackles to lift. I turned to see a fox perched on the side of an industrial wheelie bin. Another one clambered out just then and grinned at me, a blackened banana skin hanging from one ear.

'There's masses to eat in here, innit,' it said. 'Why don't you climb in and share a bite with us? We've got some wicked taco wrappers, half-eaten burgers and a couple of fish heads.'

'Fish heads?' The fox on top of the bin looked at his companion. 'Fresh fish heads?'

Even as a young *puppy*, my 'Please can I have another ham sandwich?' look was a killer.

I've always been a fan of a chill-out session.

. . . but Walking Club commitments often intervened!

With two of my siblings. Note how their human friends are cuddling them while mine stays at arm's length. Is it any wonder I was paranoid about never finding a home?

I really did try to
get involved in group
activities . . .

. . . but going outside
in this weather?

You must be
barking!

The one and only Smidgit - image reproduced by kind permission of **Go Guinea Pigs!** magazine.

Some of Smidgit's line-dancing team. Unfortunately they struggled with the concept of a line.

Obi and Indi - full of
energy and enthusiasm,
and always up for a larf.

Once I figured out how to stand (in this case with the aid of a ham sandwich in Ashleigh's hood), the sky was the limit!

But I'll always prefer to keep my feet firmly on the ground.

Agility training pays off and my rosette collection blooms!

The other fox dipped out of sight for a moment. Then it returned and shook its head.

'Nah,' he said with some excitement in his voice. 'They're well manky.'

'Why didn't you tell me, bro?' said the first fox, sounding cheated all of a sudden. 'Or was you hoping to keep the best for yourself?' They then both jumped inside.

'Hey, mind yo' manners! Take it easy. Get off! That's mine!'

I couldn't see the scrap that broke out inside the bin. Judging by the rubbish that began to arc out onto the street, I knew it wasn't something I wanted to be involved in. I moved on quickly, hoping to be out of sight by the time they came back up for air. I didn't want to share a meal with that pair. They looked totally untrustworthy. Even if they did have fish heads on offer – a delicacy Ashleigh has still never offered me to this day – I hoped I'd find supper elsewhere.

It was a thought that hit me hard. As a puppy, I had lived in fear of being flung out unwanted on the streets. Instead, Ashleigh, Penny and the pets had offered me a place in their home. It had been a wonderful life, but now I had thrown it away. And all because of a stupid, selfish dream.

When the first drops of rain began to fall, I should've looked for a place to shelter. Instead, it felt strangely refreshing. Perhaps my spirits were already at their lowest when the weather broke. Instead of making me feel wet and miserable, I looked up at the breaking storm and began to laugh. Things really couldn't get any worse for me, I decided. If I was at rock bottom, I realised, with a swing to my step, then perhaps the only way from here was up.

The rain grew heavier, every passing car kicking up puddles in my face. I wasn't going to let it dampen this strange upswing in my mood, so I hurried for the shelter of an alley between a multi-storey car park and a cinema. The rain still hammered down, but I was beyond caring any more. As I plodded around a pile of cardboard boxes, I even found myself humming a little tune. It was the first one that had ever left me spellbound, from the musical I had once watched with Penny. I remembered it was sung by a man in a downpour. All at once the sound of rain hammering all around me seemed like part of the song playing in my head. I closed my eyes as I drifted down the alley, singing along to myself, and then found my paws were no longer just padding. They were tapping in time with the tune, which only encouraged me to strut and hold my head ever higher. By the time I reached the next verse, I was doing the one thing that had led me into this fix, and I no longer cared.

I was dancing. Dancing my little dog's heart out.

I skipped sideways, one way then the other, before swirling around and around. My coat was soaked but that didn't trouble me. In my mind I was on the stage, where I'd always wanted to be. I finished the song with a short spin, and faced up to the bruising clouds. For a moment, I relished the rain on my face. Then, to my surprise, I heard what sounded like applause.

I snapped open my eyes, and realised that the sound

was caused by a mass of flapping wings. A flock of street pigeons were just coming into land at the exit to the alley. There were dozens of them, with beady eyes that fixed me from all sorts of different angles.

'Hold up there, chum,' said one pigeon, a tough-looking bird with one misshapen foot. He hobbled forward to address me. 'I don't believe you've paid the congestion charge for the area.'

'Congestion?' I looked around. 'Where?'

'The boxes,' the pigeon replied, as the others cooed behind him. 'The boxes clogging up this fine thorough-fare. It's our job to push them aside and keep the traffic flowing, but we can't do that without a fee.'

'But I don't carry any money,' I told him. 'To be honest I didn't think birds like you did either.'

The pigeon circled around me.

'So, what have you got?' he asked.

'Nothing,' I said, feeling increasingly uncomfortable.

The pigeon stopped in front of me. The rain was still beating down, but it just bounced off his feathers.

'That collar don't look like nothing,' he said. 'If it sparkles, we're interested.'

'I can't do that,' I said, and took a step backwards. 'My owner gave it to me.'

The pigeon mimicked what I had just said, in a silly voice. The flock behind him laughed.

'Lads,' he said, turning to them for a moment. 'Secure the area.'

At once, half the pigeons took to the air. They flew over my head so close I had to duck, and then settled behind me. I looked back at the ringleader. He had tipped his head to glare at me side on.

'Gimme the collar, friend. Or face the consequences.'

I was outnumbered. These streetwise feathered fiends had completely blocked my path. I looked behind me once more, and then back at the ringleader.

'Listen,' I said. 'Just let me pass. I'm a dog. In the wild, dog beats pigeon.'

This made them laugh again, louder this time.

'Dog beats pigeon,' he said. 'That's a good one.'

'I'm not joking,' I said. 'Don't make me angry.'

The pigeon twitched his head several times. Then he found me with his other eye.

'The collar,' he said menacingly. 'Or we'll just have to take it from you.'

I had heard enough. Despite being surrounded, I decided it was time to move. This wasn't such a nice place to be after all. With a warning growl, I sprang forward. The pigeon flew out of my path, only to come back around on top of me along with many of his companions. As I forced a passage through the flock, every bird attempted to peck at me. It was a horrible feeling, like being stung by a swarm of unwashed bees.

'Get off!' I cried out, and momentarily shook myself free. 'Leave me alone!'

I struggled to the end of the alley and plunged across the road. A cyclist swerved around us but with the pigeons in pursuit I didn't stop sprinting. All I could do was race into a side road and try to shake them off. It proved impossible, however. Every time I lost a bird they'd simply take to wing and dive bomb me once more.

'I warned you, friend,' warbled the ringleader, as feathers continued to fly.

I was tearing towards another junction. This one looked much busier than the last. Cars and lorries swished through the puddles one way and the other. My chances of getting across safely looked slim, but what choice did I have? Mugged by pigeons, I was being badly assaulted with no sign of any let-up. The rain was still coming down hard. The spray on the road made it even tougher for me to judge if there would be a gap.

'You're going down,' snarled the ringleader, flapping backwards through the air just ahead of me. 'Face it. Pigeon beats dog!'

By now I had no idea if there was a space in the traffic. The pigeons' beaks were really beginning to hurt and sting. If I stopped, I didn't think I would get going again. As the junction approached I even picked up my pace. I bucked and kicked in a bid to shake them off, but they kept on coming. So, squeezing my eyes shut and thinking it was now or never, I scrambled out into the road. At the same time, the sound of squealing tyres cut through the storm. I froze in the oncoming headlights. The car's horn blared, causing every pigeon to take off into the night. My time had come, I figured in a flash, and I braced myself for the impact. But the crash I expected didn't come. I felt the bumper kiss me as the vehicle came to a halt, and then a door was hurriedly opened.

'*Pudsey! Is that you?*'

I recognised her voice straight away.

'Ashleigh?' I opened one eye and looked around. When I saw her, rushing to my side with tears in her eyes, I came alive in an instant. '*Ashleigh*!'

'It's him, Mum!' she cried, and scooped me into her arms. 'We've found him! Pudsey, we've been out looking for you for hours!'

It was the last thing I expected to happen, and the only thing I could've wished for. My whole body felt sore from the attack, my bones were cold from the rain and I felt foolish for all the trouble I had caused. Still, none of that mattered to me now. As Ashleigh bundled me onto the back seat and jumped in behind me, I licked her face all over and looked forward to going home.

In my heart, I thought to myself, as I reflected on what I'd just been through, I'd never really left.

11

Paws for Thought

I'd like to correct some things that have been written about me in the media lately. I haven't started a feud with Aleksandr the meerkat. Nor have I checked into canine rehab to deal with my four-crispy-pig's-ears-a-day habit. I do wish journalists would check their facts before going to press. Those little rawhide booty chews are my big weakness at the moment. Mmmm.

I had no need for a scrub that night. Ashleigh insisted on showering me down despite my protests, but the fact was I felt cleansed. When it came to dreams, I realised I'd been living mine all along. During my time on the streets, I'd seen dogs and other animals with no home they could call their own, and with nobody who loved them. I could count on Ashleigh and a roof over my head. I couldn't ask for more.

The only downside was Handsome Brad. He seemed to be the only one who wasn't pleased and relieved to see me once again. The cruel cat found me several days later, sunning myself with the guinea pigs.

'So, you're back,' he observed, and padded along the fence. Brad looked totally unconcerned by the presence of Shredder in the garden behind us. Despite the fact that the bulldog kept hurling himself at the fence, snapping and barking with every leap, he just sat upon the ridge and looked at me disapprovingly. 'What's wrong? Too hot to dance today?'

I was stretched out on the grass, watching what was going on inside the run.

'Dancing isn't my thing any more,' I told him. 'I'm happy just watching the others strut their stuff.'

As I spoke, Smidgit had just finished arranging the others in a line. She scuttled from one end to the middle, and from there addressed them all.

'OK, listen up!' she said, only to pause until two young guinea pigs stopped poking their tongues through the fence at the bulldog and faced her. 'We'll take it from the top one more time, but don't forget we end with a double paw stomp. Not a single like some of you did just then.'

I had to give Smidgit credit. She was a great choreographer. The guinea pig observed her students closely as they ran through the sequence, as did Handsome Brad.

'Why don't we liven things up a little?' he suggested, and hopped on top of the cage. 'How about the first guinea pig to step out of line has to hop outside for a masterclass with me?'

Smidgit looked up at the cat. She seemed less than impressed.

'Don't you think you've caused enough trouble as it is?' she dared to ask him. 'Poor Pudsey could've vanished into the night for ever thanks to you.'

'Someone had to tell him straight,' said Brad. 'The dog can't dance. It's not what dogs are designed to do.'

'You destroyed his dreams,' she said, standing her ground. 'Nobody has the right to do that!'

Handsome Brad hadn't really been paying Smidgit much attention. Now, in the face of such an accusation, he narrowed his eyes and stared at her.

'You want to be careful with loose talk like that,' he warned her. 'Cats have the right to do anything they please. There are no rules for me. The only thing you need to know is cats rule.'

I'm not sure that Shredder respected Brad's views. As he

talked, the bulldog continued to make an almighty racket from behind the fence. Brad didn't seem at all bothered. He peered at every guinea pig in turn, none of them daring to respond. Only Smidgit glared back at him.

'Why does your kind have to be so nasty?' she asked. 'I had such high hopes for Pudsey!'

'I'm just here to help,' said Handsome Brad, who seemed to relish the fact that he had touched a nerve.

I had heard enough, however. All this bickering wasn't going to change a thing.

'Guys,' I said, standing up. 'We don't know how lucky we are just being here. We've got everything we need. Whether it's food, water, radiators, laps, regular walks or just simple love and affection ...' I paused there and tried to ignore Brad as he buried his head in his paws and groaned. 'Whatever you enjoy about being here, it's in our best interests if we all just learn to get along.'

I felt the impact of my stirring speech was lessened slightly by the fact that I'd had to raise my voice to be heard over next door's snarling dog, but then I wasn't addressing Shredder. He wasn't a part of the family. Nor was Brad, when I thought about it. Then again, as the cat spent more time here than in his own home I had to consider him. I'm not sure Smidgit agreed, however.

'The day that Brad apologises for the way he treated you,' she said, 'is the day we can start afresh as friends.'

'Ain't going to happen,' Brad purred quietly to himself, and went on to examine his claws.

'Listen, Pudsey,' said Smidgit, turning to address me. 'If you ever want more coaching from me then just say the word. The same goes for Indi and Obi. They're happy to help.'

'You're very sweet,' I told her, 'but it was never going to make that dream of mine come true. I love watching all of you line dance, but it's not a good look for a dog. People just think we're having trouble finding a comfortable spot to lie down. As for the collies, they like to work out to funk and punk rock. The rowdy stuff's fun, but that's not dancing. It's play fighting.'

'What about your mother?' asked Smidgit. 'She's been very supportive.'

'Oh, she has,' I agreed. 'But you know what mums are like. She says every dance I try is wonderful.'

Smidgit smiled as if she understood.

'You know what?' she said after a moment. 'Maybe you've just been looking in the wrong place for help to live your dream.'

'Really, Smidgit, I've got over it now,' I said. 'All that's in the past.'

'If we can't make it happen,' she continued, ignoring what I'd just said, 'I think we all know who you should turn to.'

By now, Brad was growing tired of all the noise that Shredder was making. He leapt back onto the fence and hissed at him.

'Will you shut up for once in your life?' he asked. 'For crying out loud, Shredder, we're having a conversation over here! This is a fence. It divides our gardens in two. That side's for savages like you, and this is the civilised side. You can spend your time crunching on bones and barking at the slightest breath of wind, we'll get on with discussing hopes and failed ambitions. The fence is designed to keep us apart, so just accept it. Barking like that's not going to change anything. Nor is jumping up every twenty seconds. It's just annoying. So cut it out, all right?'

It didn't sound as if Brad's advice was going down too well. If anything, it simply wound up Shredder even more. I could hear the psychotic pooch head-butting the fence and possibly punching his own head repeatedly with his paws. The cat just tutted and faced us once again. 'So, go on then,' he said, switching his attention between Smidgit and me. 'Even if you can find someone to help Pudsey learn to dance, where's he going to perform? There's a very good reason there's no such thing as *Strictly Come Barking*.'

'What do you care?' asked Smidgit.

'I don't …' All of a sudden, Handsome Brad realised that he'd been showing far too much interest in our conversation. 'It's just you were talking and that knuckle-head back there was making such a racket I couldn't hear myself think, let alone talk, and I've a headache and … Oh, forget it.'

'I see.' I winked at Smidgit, well aware that despite his protests, the cat was still hanging on our every word. 'Anyway, it doesn't matter who you have in mind,' I told her. 'That chapter in my life is over.'

As I found a new spot to settle, the guinea pigs heard the back door opening. I didn't notice it myself, but the outbreak of chatter and squeaking told me they hoped it meant mealtime. I glanced around and saw Ashleigh making her way towards us.

'There you are!' She crouched to pat me on the back. Whether it was first thing in the morning, the middle of the day or last thing at night, she was always pleased to see me. It meant what she had to say next left me feeling just a little bit awkward. 'It's time for our agility training. There's a big competition coming up!'

I looked up at Ashleigh. I didn't want to let her down, and so I wagged my tail to show her how exciting that sounded. I loved agility simply because it made her so happy. The dark tunnels, the heights and the balance beams still made me go weak at the knees, but I kept that to myself. As I prepared to leave with her, I glanced back to say goodbye to everyone. When I did so, I found Handsome Brad and Smidgit watching me with what seemed like the same thought in mind.

'All you have to do is let her know what you'd really like to be doing,' said Smidgit. 'If anyone can make that dream come true, it's Ashleigh.'

Handsome Brad nodded in agreement, until he realised I was watching him. Then he swatted away the suggestion and sneered.

'Don't forget to look in the mirror before you start getting ideas, Twinkle Toes,' he called after me. 'The mirror never lies!'

12

Olympic gold medallist Jessica Ennis
is just out of shot ... behind us.

I worked my heart out for Ashleigh that day and throughout the weeks that followed, doubling my efforts as the competition drew closer. She'd put everything she had into training me in agility, and so it seemed to me the only thing I could offer her. At the same time, as I plunged through tunnels, zigzagged between posts and scrambled up and down ramps, I dwelled upon Smidgit's suggestion.

Could Ashleigh really be the one who might teach me how to dance? She was certainly capable of commitment. That was unquestionable. I knew she liked to tap her toes as well. She had even been involved in a school play that featured a little dance routine. Every time she practised in her bedroom, I'd try to join in. Music, I felt sure, was the means by which I hoped she'd realise that I was a dog who wanted to dance. But my efforts only made her smile, and after a few minutes she'd insist that I watch from the bed because I was getting in her way.

'I love you, Pudsey,' she once said. 'It's just now isn't the time for games.'

I reflected on this throughout the agility competition. Ashleigh had trained me so well that I practically flew around the course. I couldn't say whether we came first, last or somewhere in between, however. By the time the prizes were announced, I was fast asleep in my travelling crate. It wasn't unusual for a dog to be worn out after such an event, but if I'm honest I wasn't in it to win it. I just wanted to make Ashleigh happy, and then settle back for an easy family life.

There was just one thing that persuaded me to act on Smidgit's advice. While Ashleigh, Penny and Grandma were holding their breath for the judges' announcement, I was lost in a vivid dream. Instead of being on the sidelines of the sports hall where the competition had taken place, I was on stage. Not only that. I was doing the one thing I believed I had left behind. Dancing, it seemed to me, was something I could never turn my back on. I couldn't even walk away from it in my sleep. And nor did I want to. Ashleigh and I had proved that we could work well as a team in one discipline. Now it was time I persuaded her to climb into her dancing shoes.

'Mum,' said Ashleigh some days later. 'Have you been looking through my CDs?'

'Not me,' said Penny, who was polishing another trophy for the cabinet.

'It's just I've found them strewn across the floor of my room.'

Penny set her cloth down for a moment.

'How strange,' she said next. 'I thought you'd been going through my musical DVDs. Someone's pulled the basket out from under the coffee table and tipped it all over the floor.'

Mother and daughter glanced at one another.

'It wouldn't be Grandma,' asked Ashleigh. 'Would it?'

Penny considered this for a moment. Then she chuckled to herself.

'It wouldn't be her,' she said. 'Maybe we've got a ghost!'

The house wasn't haunted, of course. Although I did my best to spook them, floating behind them expectantly while they joked about who might've made such a mess. I even barked when Ashleigh dismissed her mother's suggestion. I just wanted her to make the connection between music and me.

To my dismay, Ashleigh headed for the back door instead, because she figured I was asking for her to be let into the garden.

Outside, the other dogs were gathered on the lawn beside the cage. The guinea pigs looked very disappointed when I padded into view, but I didn't take it personally. It was all about mealtimes for them – except for one. When Smidgit saw me plodding towards them, she read my mind without needing to ask what was wrong.

'Never mind, Pudsey,' she said. 'We'll find a way to get the message across to her.'

'I'm not so sure.' I settled beside my mum and the collies. 'All I've managed to do so far is make the house untidy.'

Shredder sounded like he was in fierce form on the other side of the garden fence. It didn't help that some of the guinea pigs were positioned at the knotholes, flicking wood shavings at him.

'Where's Handsome Brad?' I asked the other dogs.

Obi gestured along the street.

'Some new people have moved in,' he said.

'Brad's carrying out a quality assessment,' added Indi. 'If it turns out to be a better place than this one, he'll move in himself.'

'I see,' I said. 'Well, I'd be sorry to see him go.'

'Really?' Mum was dozing in the sun, but her ears pricked when I said this. 'But he's made your life a misery.'

'Brad can be a challenge,' I admitted. 'But we'd never get anywhere in life without a challenge.'

'Wise words for a dog so young.' This was Smidgit. She had brushed her coat differently, I thought. Maybe she'd used hairspray or something, because it was flicked up stylishly at the front. Then I took a closer look and realised she must have been facing the wind for a while. 'That's why you shouldn't give up on Ashleigh,' she continued. 'Somehow, we'll find a way to make her realise that you're born to dance. Isn't that right, guys?'

Obi, Indi and my mum were quick to back her up. I just wasn't sure how they would get the message across.

Over the following days, I was to find that if a dog's intelligence could be measured by its sense of loyalty, we'd be the smartest creatures on the planet. Unfortunately, as I discovered from the efforts my friends made to communicate with Ashleigh, it didn't work like that.

'How come you two aren't eating?' I asked one morning, on finding Obi and Indi at their feed bowl. I had wolfed down my breakfast in a matter of seconds. According to dog law, our dry food would spoil if exposed to fresh air for more than a minute. 'You really need to hurry up.'

'It's OK,' said Obi. 'We're sacrificing our breakfast for you.'

'Observe,' Indi chipped in, before upturning the bowl across the tiles. 'We may not be able to pick up a pen, but we can position the kibble into a clear message.'

I watched them begin to shove one meaty nugget after another with their noses. I was a little lost for words. In a way, the same could be said for Obi and Indi.

'I really appreciate what you're doing for me here,' I said after a moment, 'but aren't you overlooking one thing?'

'What's that?' asked Obi, stepping back to check his work.

'We can't write,' I said. That drew their attention. 'None of us can. A dog would have to be exceptionally talented to learn how to write or even read. We'd be talking about a one of a kind!'

Indi looked back at the floor.

'But it says "Ashleigh: please teach Pudsey to dance", doesn't it?'

I tipped my head to one side, struggling to catch up with what was going on here.

'That's what you want it to say,' I assured them. 'But really it's just a mess of kibble.'

'How do you know,' asked Obi, 'if dogs can't read or write?'

I drew breath to answer, only to find I had no explanation. The collies were clearly bonkers, but their way of thinking had left me questioning my sanity. At the same time, a low chuckle from the kitchen sideboard told us that Handsome Brad had materialised. Sometimes nobody saw him slip into the house. We could turn, as we did just then, and find him watching us as if he'd been there for some time.

'Pudsey's right,' he told the collies. 'You've just wasted your breakfast.'

'Really?' Obi exchanged a worried glance with Indi. 'Do you think there's still time to eat it up before it goes stale?'

'Here goes nothing!' she declared, and prepared to find out for herself.

I stood well back while Indi and Obi frantically hunted down every last kibble. Handsome Brad looked down upon the scene and shook his head.

'Dogs never fail to amaze me,' he said. 'You're beyond stupid!'

My mum had also been watching the collies and me from her basket. Hearing the cat mock us, she lifted her head to address him.

'At least they tried to help Pudsey,' she said. 'Now it's my turn.'

'How?' I asked.

'You'll see,' Mum said, with such confidence I almost thought it came with a guarantee.

We didn't have to wait long. As always, whenever Penny spent time in the kitchen, the first thing she did was switch on the radio. I was in my basket at the time, while the collies dozed on their pillow beside me. That didn't last long, however, because my mum climbed to her feet at the first sound of music and began to sing along.

'Quick,' she said at the end of the first verse. 'Dance, Pudsey. Dance!'

'What? Why?'

I looked across at the collies, who had stirred at the dreadful howling that Mum was making. Even Penny looked concerned.

'What's the matter?' she asked, as Mum continued to wail. 'Is it a cramp?'

'We've got her attention,' my mum hissed from the side of her mouth. 'Now's your chance!'

'Mum, it just sounds like you're in pain,' I tried to tell her. 'Dogs can't sing, remember?'

By now, Penny had heard enough. While Mum continued to caterwaul, she rushed from the kitchen and came back with her car keys.

'Come on, old girl,' she said, and heaved Mum into her arms. 'Let's get you to the vet.'

People depend on dogs for lots of things. We provide security and companionship. We're loyal and loving. Some of us can even be trained to help people in need. There are lots of things that dogs can do. Unfortunately, when it comes to singing we sound like something the cat's dragged in.

I chose not to tell Handsome Brad about what my mum had done. She had my best interests at heart, after all. But I wished she had warned me so that I could've talked her out of it. Instead, when she returned with a clean bill of health, I told him that she'd been for her annual check-up.

'I think we both know that doesn't involve an IQ test,' Brad said with a smirk.

I had found him in his usual spot on the fence behind the guinea pigs' run. As ever, Shredder's ears could be seen flapping up and down in the background as he repeatedly made a bid to snatch the cat in his jaws. As for the noise, it sounded as if the neighbours kept a feral zombie back there.

'Everyone's just trying their best,' I told him over the din. 'It might've got us nowhere, but I'm touched that they've made such an effort.'

'Which is more than can be said for you,' squeaked a voice from inside the run directed at Brad. Smidgit had left the shed to scold the younger guinea pigs, who had been daring each other to poke their tails through the knotholes in the fence. Having hauled them back she turned to me and volunteered her services in my bid to bring Ashleigh up to speed. 'We're happy to help you, Pudsey. At least some of us around here want to see you succeed.'

Brad seemed most amused that the guinea pigs believed that they could make my dream come true. As the other dogs had tried and failed to inform Ashleigh of what I really wanted to perform, however, I figured I had nothing to lose.

'So, what's the plan?' I asked.

Smidgit gestured at the herd of guinea pigs behind her.

'We might've kept our passion for line dancing a secret, but now it's time to show Penny and Ashleigh what we can do. All you have to do is join in with us, Pudsey. They'll work out the rest.'

'Hello? Can I point out something here?' All of us turned to face Handsome Brad. 'If they discover guinea pigs can line dance then you guys can expect a whole lot of attention,' he said, 'and not just from Penny and Ashleigh. The world would want to see you in action. In fact, there's a very good chance that Pudsey'll be completely overlooked.'

Smidgit thought about this for a moment. Then she batted her lashes and turned to me.

'Ashleigh only has eyes for you,' she said. 'It's just every time you've tried to dance for her before you've been missing something really important.'

'What's that?' I asked.

'Direction!' declared Smidgit, only for the sound of the back door opening to draw her attention. 'And now's your chance to shine, Pudsey!'

Before I could protest that we might need more time to get things right, Smidgit began hurrying the guinea pigs into position.

'On the count of three, OK? Let's make this one special, everyone!'

This was it, I realised. All of a sudden, it seemed like it

was my last-ditch attempt to show Penny and Ashleigh that I really believed I had a future in dance. Smidgit picked a sequence that we had all practised many times. It was a tough one, which involved facing in four different directions. Still, we all knew the drill. Even Brad looked grudgingly impressed as we fell into formation, before slinking off as Penny and Ashleigh, accompanied by Grandma, appeared on the lawn. As the three approached, Smidgit got things going in the run behind the bush. I kept in step and time, mirroring their moves.

It didn't last long. I can only think the prospect of being fed caused all the guinea pigs but one to break their concentration. Within seconds, they were squealing madly while dashing about at random. Only Smidgit continued with the sequence on her own, well aware that I needed her guidance if this was to stand a chance of working.

'Pudsey?' said Ashleigh, who spotted me turning one way and the other. 'Is everything OK?'

'Front left paw forward,' squeaked Smidgit. 'Rear right back.'

I wasn't going to stop now, even when Penny bent down to take a closer look at me.

'Something isn't right with these dogs at the moment,' she observed. 'Pudsey seems disturbed.'

Like every other attempt, I could see this one ending in failure and a possible trip to the vet. Tears of frustration began to well in my eyes. Even so, I carried on following Smidgit's instructions. I couldn't even see her among the scrum of squealing, hungry guinea pigs. Ashleigh and Penny weren't paying them any attention. Even Grandma was looking directly at me. She had hung back a little bit, but when she spoke even the squeaks fell away.

'Do you know what I think he's doing?' she said. Penny and Ashleigh turned around. Grandma smiled and pointed at me. 'That dog is trying to dance!'

13

Paws for Thought

It's a little-known fact that dogs have
up to one hundred different facial expressions.
Handsome Brad will tell you that Obi and Indi
have mastered just one. He says nobody does
'stupidity' like they do. As for me, I'm a
natural at doing 'happy', 'dreamy' . . .
well, that's one more than the collies!

Some time passed before Handsome Brad slunk back to visit us. His pride had clearly taken quite a knock when he found out about our news. When he eventually showed up, Ashleigh had already switched our training routine. Instead of clattering over the agility course all the time, we now took a portable stereo with us. It was Ashleigh who had said out loud that it might be fun to do something together that involved music. She had no idea just what had gone into leading her to believe it was her idea, nor how much it meant to me, but my enthusiasm was evident. From there on, we went right back to basics, and began to explore a way that we could dance together.

'Look at you two,' Brad said, just after Ashleigh and I had finished a session in the back garden. He was sitting on the side fence. I figured he had been watching for some time. 'It's the most ridiculous thing I've seen in my life. Even more ridiculous than line-dancing guinea pigs. Pudsey, where's your self-respect?'

'Hi, Brad,' I said, deliberately ignoring his comments. 'We were wondering what you'd been up to.'

'The new people have been feeding me titbits from the table.' The ginger tom cleaned his whiskers. 'Everything was cool until they caught me peeing under their little boy's bed. Now I'm back to reclaim some radiators.'

'I see.' I padded across the grass and sat before him.

'Well, you haven't missed much. Ashleigh and I have just been doing a lot of practising.'

'Passion and practice,' said Brad, nodding. 'Same goes for catching mice.'

I was still a little breathless from working out with Ashleigh. I had been learning how to dash in between her legs as she walked. We were making good progress. It was all about finding a way to work with each other, so that we danced as one. What's more, it wasn't just me who appeared to love every moment. Ashleigh seemed equally thrilled.

'We're a team,' I told him. 'And I've got all of you to thank.'

'Me?' Brad opened his eyes wide. 'Oh, come on!'

'That day you asked me to dance in front of the mirror?' I said. 'It nearly destroyed my dream, and drove me out onto the streets, but you know what? I feel like I came home stronger.'

'Well, that's great,' said Brad begrudgingly. 'Can we just keep this a secret? If the neighbourhood cats find out there's a dancing dog in my pack, I'll never live it down. This really isn't how I should be rolling.'

'Oh, this is just the beginning,' I told him. 'Ashleigh and I are going places.'

'No kidding. Where are you off to?'

I hadn't actually considered where exactly we were going. It was just something I had in mind. Judging by the way Brad grinned at me, he could tell I had no idea.

'I'm sure if you keep working you and Ashleigh will be able to put on a good show for the family at Christmas.'

'That would be nice,' I said, 'but I'm aiming higher than that.'

The ginger tom jumped into the garden and headed for the back door.

'Well, once your sights are set then come and ask me for permission. Until then, I'll be in my crib.'

'Do you mean the airing cupboard?' I asked just to check. 'Fourth shelf down on the fluffy towels?'

'That's what I said,' he grumbled. 'My crib.'

My conversation with Brad left me thinking. I had dreamed of becoming a dancing dog, but now that dream was taking shape I didn't know where to go with it. Ashleigh was completely focused on taking me through a range of commands, and I loved her for it. But I was concerned that if we didn't find a stage to put on a show then she might grow tired of training me.

'It's good to be driven,' said Indi one evening. 'Without drive, you just become a fat, lazy dog who does nothing but lounge around.'

We were gathered in the front room. It was an unseasonably chilly night, and so Penny had lit the fire. As soon as she did so, a scrum took place among the dogs to win prime position on the hearth. Obi and Indi had won out, and were both sprawled upon their backs.

'It's about commitment, guts, courage and hard work,' added Obi, stopping there to stretch and yawn.

'Are you prepared to take things to the limit?' Indi

asked me with all four legs in the air. 'Do you reckon you've got what it takes?'

My mum was sitting behind them. Unlike the collies, she had yet to surrender to the blissful heat from the fire. Still, the irony of what they were saying wasn't lost on her.

'No doubt Pudsey benefits from sharing a house with two fine athletes such as you,' she told them.

'I should hope so,' said Obi with a sigh, and promptly closed his eyes.

'Some of us have to set an example,' Indi added, twisting one way and then the other to scratch her back.

Penny, Ashleigh and Grandma were finishing supper in the kitchen. Ashleigh had been watching television with us, and had left the set on when Penny called her through for her dinner.

'Oh, look,' Brad said from his favourite armchair. 'It's that *Britain's Gone Bananas* show.'

'What show?' I asked, unaware that the cat had even joined us.

'You know? The one where people perform stuff in front of a panel of judges. They go on it thinking they've got a special act, but sometimes it's just, well, not so special.'

Mum returned her attention to the screen.

'It's called *Britain's Got Talent*,' she said. 'And I think you're being harsh, Brad. It takes courage to step up in front of an audience, no matter what you have to offer. Besides, a lot of the acts are really good!'

Brad sneered dismissively.

'I only watch it for the tears and the heartbreak,' he said. 'It gives me a warm and cuddly feeling inside.'

For a moment, we all sat quietly as a man dressed as a knight stood behind a table and chopped wood in time to music. I glanced at Brad. Judging by the look on his face, the act completely justified everything he had just said. I thought it was a brave and impressive skill, but said nothing – I didn't want to earn the cat's derision. Instead, it was Obi who broke the silence, which he did by breaking wind.

'Oh, for goodness' sake!' my mum grumbled. 'Being a dog really shouldn't be an excuse.'

'Sorry,' said Obi, and shifted position in front of the fire. 'Penny bought us some new chews recently. Blame her.'

Handsome Brad looked disgusted.

'Epic blow-offs are about your only talent, Obi. Somehow I doubt you'd get far on a show like this.'

Obi rolled over and looked up at the cat.

'I can do a lot of things that would impress those judges,' he said, sounding a little affronted. 'Speed eating, for example.'

'Squirrel chasing,' added Indi. 'You're good at that.'

'If it was me,' Mum said, 'I'd sing.'

'I'm sure we can think of something else you're good at,' I told her hurriedly. 'Although of course your voice is lovely.'

Handsome Brad listened with interest.

'Maybe you and Ashleigh should audition for the show,' he suggested. 'I for one would love to see you embarrass yourselves on national television.'

Indi's ears pricked at the suggestion.

'That's not a bad idea,' she said. 'You could dance for the judges!'

'I was joking,' said Brad before I could draw breath. 'I don't suppose they even allow dogs into the building.'

'Come on, all of you,' I said, 'joke or no joke, *Britain's Got Talent* is way out of our league. I wouldn't dream of putting Ashleigh through the pain. It's true I've got high hopes. It's just I was thinking along the lines of something a bit more, well, local. Amateur dramatics, maybe?' Obi, Indi and my mum looked at me as if perhaps they were hoping I would change my mind. 'No way!' I added, laughing now. 'It's out of the question. End of story!'

14

'Some of my best leading men have been dogs.'
Elizabeth Taylor

I was quick to forget all about the other pets' proposal. At least I would've done had they stopped needling me about it throughout the weeks that followed. Every Saturday, during *Britain's Got Talent*, the collies would observe that Ashleigh and I could do better. According to Obi, the gymnastic troupe called Spelbound who had won the previous year weren't only missing a letter in their name. They were also lacking a dog. At the same time, Indi kept pointing out that New Bounce would never appreciate the true meaning of the word without an excitable canine among them. Honestly, they would go on to raise the subject before and after every single dancing session. If we rehearsed in the garden, they'd even come and watch.

'That would look good on TV,' observed Indi on one occasion. 'Wouldn't it look good, Obi?'

I had just learned how to jump through Ashleigh's arms. As soon as she formed a hoop for me, I took my cue and leapt.

'It wouldn't just look good,' observed Obi. 'It would look terrific! Pudsey, this is showbiz gold. Pure entertainment! I can picture it now. Your name in lights!'

I tried hard to ignore them. Dancing with Ashleigh took real concentration. Most important of all, she always hid a little treat for me in one hand, pressed between her thumb and her palm. I kept my eye on that every step of the way, and followed it wherever she took me.

'Well done!' she declared, when I jumped clean through her arms, waited for her to spin around and then repeated the trick a second time. 'Here, you deserve this!'

The other dogs watched with envy as I crunched on the treat.

'If I could dance like you,' said Mum, 'I'd want to share it with the nation.'

'It's a lovely idea,' I said when I had finished. 'But what if it all went wrong? I couldn't bear to think that I might be responsible for embarrassing Ashleigh.'

'I really don't think that would happen,' Indi assured me. 'It's shaping up to be a very impressive act.'

Even at the bottom of the garden, there was no escape from the nagging.

'You're a natural,' said Smidgit. 'Us guinea pigs are just too timid for the stage, so I'm pleased our secret's still safe. We were prepared to risk it for you, Pudsey, and look how it's turned out! Now that you're getting coaching from Ashleigh, you've improved leaps and bounds. And I mean that quite literally.'

I was sitting with my front paws touching the wire of their run. As usual, the younger guinea pigs were devoting their day to driving Shredder wild.

'But even if I came round to the idea,' I said, 'how would we persuade Ashleigh to audition? Making her realise I liked to dance was one thing. Asking her to try out for the show would be impossible!'

Smidgit backed up a bit, as if to consider me from a distance.

'Are you saying you'd think about giving it a shot?'

'No,' I told her. 'No way.'

'Because if you are,' she said with alarming certainty, 'I'm sure we can find a way.'

For once, I was in agreement with Handsome Brad. My dream of dancing stopped well short of stepping on stage on a national television show.

'Within seconds, you'd be branded for the rest of your life as one deluded dog,' he said. 'I think you should audition at the earliest opportunity.'

I rolled my eyes, but grinned despite myself. I was lying at the foot of the landing radiator. Brad was draped across the top. It wasn't switched on but the sunshine at that time of day was intense in that particular spot.

'I'm sure you'd love to see that,' I told him. 'But I'm happy as I am.'

'No you're not,' he said. 'You're obviously itching to show the world what you can do. It's Ashleigh who's holding you back.'

'She's not holding me back,' I said. 'I wouldn't be dancing like I am today without her help and guidance.'

'Ashleigh's a grown-up girl now,' he said. 'If she didn't want to audition for the show I'm sure she'd speak up. You just need to find a way to get her to consider it.'

Handsome Brad was half dozing in the sunshine. I glanced up at him, surprised that he would see things this way. I could only think that the heat had baked his head. I figured I'd double check anyway.

'I'd certainly feel a lot better if we did find a way to put the idea in her head. Thanks, Brad. You're a good friend.'

This served to bring Brad to his senses. He rose into a seated position and looked down at me disdainfully.

'You don't want to listen to a cat enjoying some down-time,' he said quickly. 'My brain's not in gear. Forget about the auditions. Get on with being a dog. Loyal and stupid.'

I didn't reply, but all I could think was that just a moment before, Handsome Brad might have spoken from his soul.

The next time Ashleigh and I had dancing practice, she decided the time was right to try something new. We were back in the garden with my regular audience, and none of the dogs would shut up about *Britain's Got Talent*. Handsome Brad had unwittingly softened my reluctance to audition, but I still didn't feel it was the right thing to do. Yes, Ashleigh and I could put on a little performance, but for all the jumps and twirls, I felt we lacked the 'X' factor.

As I was to discover, all that was about to change.

'Look what I've got for you, Pudsey,' she said, and opened her hand in front of me. Just one sniff told me what it was. Even the other dogs could pick up the scent.

'A ham sandwich!' Obi declared. 'Can you believe it? Who knew dancing and food went together? Hey, Ashleigh, teach me something! Teach me!'

'Quieten down,' said Ashleigh. 'All that barking's only going to put Pudsey off.'

Like all the dogs, I adored a ham sandwich as much as I adored Ashleigh herself. Just then, I was prepared to do anything for that little square of meat in a fold of bread that she'd shown me in the palm of her hand. Had she asked me to cross burning coals, I'd have given it my best shot. What she did ask me to do carried no risk of scalded paws. Even so, it was a challenge. Climbing onto the low patio wall, she held out the offering as if I was a seal in a pool.

'Go for it!' shouted Indi. 'Get the sandwich, get the sandwich!'

I jumped instinctively, only for Ashleigh to lift her hand at the last moment.

'Harsh,' said Obi. 'I think she wants you to try a different technique.'

'Like what?' I asked, bemused.

'Just do what comes naturally,' my mum advised.

I looked at Ashleigh and then at the offering in her hand. She was watching me intently, whispering words of encouragement. I closed my eyes for a moment, just to find some space to think about what it was she wanted me to do. Listening to Ashleigh, and with only the smell of the sandwich to guide me, I let something deeper take over. Without further thought, I pushed up hard on my front paws and took the weight of my body on my hind legs. I heard gasps from the other dogs as I focused on keeping my balance, and when I stretched upwards I found my treat.

'You did it, Pudsey!'

I opened my eyes and looked around. The other dogs seemed dumbstruck, while Ashleigh clapped her hands in delight.

'What did I do exactly?' I asked, and dropped back down onto all fours.

'Man,' said Obi, who had yet to blink. 'Seems you crossed over to the human side for a moment.'

'My boy,' said Mum proudly. 'You've just learned how to stand.'

Each time we rehearsed, I practised my new trick, learning to do it on command instead of for a treat. It wasn't quite the same, but I recognised that we had to think of my waistline. I even mastered how to do it in time to music, and later take my first steps. Naturally, Handsome Brad fell about laughing when I showed him, but I hoped that privately he was impressed. And all the time, the dogs and Smidgit the guinea pig continued to badger me about sharing our skills on the screen.

'It should be you up there,' Indi said, the next time we had gathered to watch *Britain's Got Talent*. It was the final. The set looked bigger and flashier than ever before, while some seriously eye-catching acts were competing to win.

'Maybe so,' I said, nestled at the foot of the sofa. 'But ultimately it's Ashleigh's decision.'

Ashleigh liked the show as much as we did, and Penny was also a big fan. Even Grandma came round to watch it. None of them had ever suggested entering, however. After the lengths we'd gone to to demonstrate I could dance, I saw no way that we could communicate my interest in auditioning. The week before, Obi had tried barking at the television and promptly been sent out. I think even Mum had realised that singing wasn't the way forward, and so we were free to enjoy the acts perform one final time before the public reached its decision. As ever, it proved to be a claw-biting finale, and emotional too when it was announced that Jai McDowall had beaten little Ronan Parke. Even Handsome Brad looked close to shedding a tear from his spot out of sight behind the armchair.

'Are you about to cry?' Indi asked him. 'Look everyone, Brad's welling up.'

'No I'm not!' he said fiercely. 'Anyway, I'm out of here.'

In his hurry to get away, if only to spare his blushes, he trotted across the remote control that was lying on the floor beside him. It was only apparent that his paw had hit a button when the television picture froze. Brad responded by high-tailing it from the front room before he was spotted.

'Who pressed pause?' asked Penny, and looked around.

Ashleigh peered under the cushion beside her and shrugged. Only Grandma continued to stare at the TV. She was looking at a freeze-frame full of words that had appeared just as the credits rolled. As we were about to learn, it contained details of an invitation that would change our lives for ever.

'You should read that, Ashleigh,' Grandma said. 'Maybe it's something you'd like to do with Puds?'

'Mum,' Ashleigh said, excitedly. 'What do you think about Pudsey and me auditioning for the next series?'

Penny had just found the remote on the carpet. She sat up and read the information for potential applicants on the screen.

'I don't know ...' she said, which prompted every pet to hold their breath. 'If you want to have a go then I don't see why not, but I suppose it really depends on whether it appeals to Pudsey.'

She didn't need to say any more. Nor did the dogs. In response, I jumped up from in front of the sofa and turned around to face Ashleigh. Then, without a command from her, I rose onto my hind legs and lifted my front paws high.

'I'm in!' I barked at her, bouncing on the spot. 'Let's do this thing, Ashleigh. I'm in! I'm in! I'm in!'

15

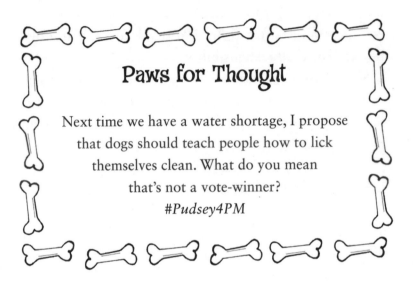

Paws for Thought

Next time we have a water shortage, I propose
that dogs should teach people how to lick
themselves clean. What do you mean
that's not a vote-winner?
#Pudsey4PM

This was one of the happiest moments of my life. Nothing could come close, even that time I rolled in fox poo shortly before the dog show at Ashleigh's school fete one year. And I had Brad to thank for it. Naturally, the cat denied all responsibility.

'So I pressed a button,' he protested. 'I didn't force Penny to get online and apply to go on the show. She did that of her own free will, with Ashleigh at her side. None of that was down to me.'

'You're right,' said Mum, with a knowing look at me. 'It had nothing to do with Brad.'

Whatever the ginger tom liked to think, there was no going back for me. From the moment Penny pressed SEND, on the closing day for applications, Ashleigh and I set out to work on our skills so that we would be fit for the show. Of course, we didn't think we stood a chance of being asked to audition. Part of me thought the producers would take one look at our submission form and throw it in the bin. Who would want to see a dog dance? I asked myself. Usually following a conversation with the cat.

'Don't listen to Brad,' said Smidgit one day, and beckoned me closer to the cage. 'You know he's jealous, don't you? He likes to be the centre of attention, and now you've taken that away from him.'

'Not on purpose,' I pointed out. 'Ashleigh and I are determined to be at the top of our game. Even if we don't receive a letter inviting us to the audition, it's something to work towards.'

Smidgit looked one way and then the other, as if to be sure we couldn't be overheard.

'The other day,' she said in a whisper, 'I saw Brad by the garden fence over there. He clearly didn't think anyone could see him because he was trying to stand on his hind legs.'

'Really?' I lifted my head. 'How did he get on?'

'Hopeless,' Smidgit told me. 'He looked like a one-cat Mexican wave. More importantly, Pudsey, it proved you really do have something special. So don't let him put you off. Keep on practising. We're right behind you!'

Several months into repeating every trick in our book, Ashleigh announced that it was time we put a routine together. To do so, we would need a soundtrack. Obi, Indi and Mum each had a suggestion to make.

'"Who Let the Dogs Out?"' said Obi. 'No question. What else is there?'

'"Hound Dog",' Mum suggested. 'I love Elvis.'

'"Beware of the Dog",' Indi chipped in. 'You'd give Jamelia a run for her money.'

I wasn't so sure about any of their suggestions. I liked a show tune. Ashleigh and I wanted to strut our stuff. I followed her upstairs, where she began to go through her

CD collection. She walked her fingers over case after case, rejecting each one in turn.

'Not that one. This one's too fast ... too slow ... too sad ... This one!'

I watched with interest as she hauled out her choice and held it up for me to see. I had no idea what it was, of course, but when she played it for me the song sounded just perfect to my ears. We were all familiar with *The Flintstones*. It had been one of Ashleigh's favourite cartoons when she was younger. In particular, we liked Dino the dinosaur who was treated like a pet dog, while the music was second to none. Ashleigh had opted for the movie soundtrack. It was a re-recording of the original by an uplifting party rock band called the B52s. As soon as I heard the opening verse, I knew she had made the right choice. It was big, full of swagger and fun. In fact, during that first play, Ashleigh and I jumped about her bedroom together as if we were in a world of our own.

Then the hard work began.

Let me tell you, it's a miracle we didn't grow sick of that song. We rehearsed to it so many times that the whole family soon knew the words.

'My poor ears!' complained Brad. 'Any more of this and they'll start bleeding.'

'It won't be for ever,' I assured him, as I went through the part of the routine where I walked behind Ashleigh with my paws on her behind. 'What do you think of us now, eh?'

'What do I think?' he said, observing from the fence. 'I think you should've picked a tune that wouldn't turn to torture after we've heard it a few times. '"Cat on a Hot

Tin Roof". "Love Cats". "Cat Scratch Fever". Anything by the Stray Cats, or Catatonia. Something that speaks to us all, you know?'

Even the guinea pigs succumbed to the endless repetition of the song. Eventually, they worked out a line dance for it. They would've made great show dancers, turning this way and that in the background with tinsel collars and all sorts, but Smidgit was having none of it.

'This is about you two,' she insisted. 'Take my advice. Even when you think the routine is perfect, keep on practising until it's even better! But above all, make sure you both enjoy what you do. It has to be fun, because that's how you'll shine.'

Ashleigh and I both made sacrifices during this time. Such was our determination to be ready, just in case the invitation arrived, we gave up some important things in our lives. After school, rather than hanging out with friends, Ashleigh came straight home. Once her homework was done, rehearsals would begin. She missed out on parties just to rehearse, which was asking a lot from a teenage girl. As for me, I was forced to turn my back on the treats, from crispy pigs' ears to rawhide bones, that Grandma always brought us dogs. I had to think of my figure. I've always had a decent metabolism, but couldn't afford to take any chances. Being a dancer demanded that I stay trim.

My worries, though, continued to get the better of me. Once, in my sleep, I dreamed that I had packed on loads of weight, just as we were asked to attend an audition. With no time to diet, and discovering that I was too large to squeeze through the front door, Ashleigh had to hoist me through the window and transport me there in a wheelbarrow. Needless to say, the response when I waddled on stage was less than supportive. It was a nightmare I didn't wish to repeat. Instead, I went on to dream that my entire canine coat fell off just as soon as the stage lights went up.

'It's natural to be nervous,' my mum assured me as we settled in one night. I was wary about going to sleep in case I had another bad dream. At the same time, I was so exhausted from all the training that I knew once I shut my eyes that would be it.

Sure enough, that night I went down deep, and dreamed of absolutely nothing. Even so, when I woke up I still felt utterly drained.

During school hours, I was free to be a lazy dog like any other. It was only when Ashleigh came home that I became a dancer. So, when Penny popped out to pick up some dry cleaning, she left us in the kitchen with the radio on. We were dozing at the time, just kicking back and doing nothing, which was how we liked it when home alone. As ever, we had the cat for company, of course. Handsome Brad knew how to find his way inside. Even though Penny had locked the doors, he'd always find an open window somewhere around the house.

'What time do you call this then?' he asked, padding into the kitchen. 'It's a sorry sight, guys. We cats don't even go to bed at night. We're outside on the prowl, keeping you safe from intruders.'

'That's our job,' Mum said sleepily. 'Burglars don't tend to break into houses where there are dogs inside.'

Handsome Brad hopped up onto the kitchen counter. Penny would have a fit if she ever found out about this, but the cat made sure he was invisible to human eyes.

'I wasn't talking about burglars with stripy tops and swag bags,' he said a little too calmly. Clearly he was irritated. 'Without me, this house would be under siege from mice. I sacrifice my nights to keep you safe. But when I do retire to a radiator, at least I know I've made a valuable contribution to society.'

Brad sounded like he was hoping for a medal from the Queen or something, but I was too exhausted to point this out. I just heaved a sigh and tried to get more shuteye.

It wasn't a problem to sleep through the radio. I was used to living with music, after all. What I couldn't ignore, however, was something that had never happened since we'd started rehearsals. It kicked in right after the news, and needed no introduction. As soon as I heard the first bar of the *Flintstones* theme tune, as played by the B52s, instinct took over. Not my canine instinct to ignore it completely, but my instinct as a dancer.

'There's no escape!' complained Handsome Brad, only to look on in surprise like everyone else when I sprang from my basket.

Even without Ashleigh, I knew every step inside out. I was barely awake, but that didn't matter. I didn't need to wait for my eyes to adjust. This was coming from the heart.

'Go for it, Pudsey!' cried Indi, with a woof that sounded more like a whoop.

For the next few minutes, I covered all four corners of the kitchen as I ran through our routine. I ignored the feline groans coming from the counter, and relished the appreciative whistles and stamping of paws from the dogs. When the song came to an end, I would normally jump into Ashleigh's arms. By that point, I was so locked inside the routine that I sprang for the first thing I could see, which happened to be the counter where Handsome Brad was perched.

'What the—' I didn't hear what the cat had to say next, on account of the fact that I had just landed on top of him. Eventually, from underneath me, I heard him say: 'For your own safety, I suggest you get off me right now.'

I did as he asked, and jumped down to the floor.

'Sorry,' I said. 'I got a bit carried away.'

The other dogs were looking on, transfixed.

'That was awesome,' said Obi eventually, and looked around at Indi. 'We should've taped that. A dog jumping into the arms of a cat. That's a guaranteed YouTube sensation!'

Brad brushed himself down. He looked furious.

'Well, that's one of my nine lives I won't be getting back,' he muttered. 'Whatever possessed you?'

I glanced around at the others. 'The music,' I said. 'The soundtrack to our performance. That's what possessed me, Brad, because right now I feel ready.'

'It was paw perfect, Pudsey,' my mum said. 'And I'm sure Brad will agree that you certainly have what it takes to be a star.'

16

I've said it before and I'll say it again:
I DO NOT APPRECIATE BEING DRESSED UP.
No matter how much I'm supposed to be
demonstrating goodwill to all men.

As Christmas approached that year, Ashleigh had just one thing on her wish list. Unfortunately, it wasn't something that anybody in the family could conjure up for her. Not without a huge amount of hard work and a little bit of luck. Gradually, we all began to worry that she might spend the festive season feeling crushed.

'So, these auditions?' my mum asked one Friday. 'When do we find out whether or not you've been selected?'

'Today's the last opportunity,' I said with a sigh. 'I just heard Penny on the phone telling Grandma. Apparently, invitations for the auditions have been going out this week. If we haven't received a letter by today, the show's over for us before it's even begun.'

Mum tried to hide her concern.

'Well, I'm sure the postman will bring good news when he arrives.'

'Ashleigh's met him at the front gate every morning this week,' I said.

My mum eyed the collies.

'How about Obi and Indi? They hate the postman.'

'They made a pact between them not to give him a hard time until after today's delivery.' I said. 'Then it's open season.'

Ashleigh and Penny were stringing Christmas cards to

hang from the walls. The postman had yet to arrive that morning. He was due at any time. It was clear that Ashleigh was tense.

'If you two are rejected,' my mum said, 'this could be the worst Christmas we've ever had.'

'Maybe the idea of a dancing dog just doesn't appeal,' I said with a sigh. 'I can't bear the thought of having built Ashleigh's hopes up only to let her down.'

'It'll be worse than that.' We turned to find Handsome Brad had slipped into the house. He was stationed under the sideboard, out of eyeshot from everyone but us. 'You'll let Ashleigh down, you'll let yourself down, and you'll let us down too. Pudsey, you'll let everyone down. I wouldn't be surprised if it's your last Christmas here, in fact.'

'A dog isn't just for Christmas,' Mum reminded him. 'Everyone knows that.'

'Oh, talk to the paw,' Brad replied. 'My point is there's a lot riding on your shoulders here.'

The atmosphere that morning was too tense for a dog nap. Everyone kept busy, but all eyes and ears were primed for the arrival of just one thing. It was Ashleigh who spotted the postman's van, even though Brad claimed to have heard him making his deliveries several minutes earlier.

'I'm all ears,' he told us from under the sideboard. 'What's more, I have a feline feeling that you're about to be massively disappointed.'

As soon as the van stopped outside the house, Ashleigh rushed to the door, accompanied by Obi and Indi. I couldn't face it, while my mum stayed behind for my sake.

'Whatever happens,' she whispered, as Penny stepped across to the window, 'you've done your best.'

'Just not enough to be selected,' came a catty voice from behind us, but we chose to ignore it.

By now, Ashleigh was rushing along the path to the gate. I could see the postman waving a clutch of envelopes. She took them from him and headed back along the path with the collies at her side, sorting them as she went.

One look at Ashleigh's expression when she appeared in the kitchen once more told us everything.

'There's no letter.' Ashleigh hung her head. 'Pudsey and I haven't made it.'

'Who saw that coming?' asked Brad quietly. 'Oh, yeah. I did.'

'Never mind, sweetheart.' Penny collected the post from her and held her gently by the shoulders. 'It was worth a try.'

I could see that Ashleigh was trying to put a brave face on things. I was gutted too, but it's a dog's duty to offer comfort at tough times. It works in the same way that a cat is expected to be cold and heartless in the face of a sensitive situation. I trotted across to Ashleigh and jumped into her arms. It was a trick we had practised to perfection. After all our hard work, it really had become second nature to us both. In a way, it made dealing with rejection that much tougher.

'I'm sorry, Pudsey,' she said, and wrapped her arms around me. 'I shouldn't have put you through all this.'

I wanted to set her straight there and then. I was the one who had put the idea in her head, after all. There was no need for Ashleigh to feel guilty. Not when the weight of responsibility was resting on my shoulders. All I could do was nuzzle her ear and hope that I hadn't ruined Christmas for her. Even Handsome Brad could see that now was not the time for a cutting remark. I glanced at him under the sideboard. He looked as if he really didn't want to be in the room, but could find no way out. The silence was uncomfortable, almost suffocating, until it was broken by a knock at the window that made us all jump.

The postman looked taken aback by our response. Through the glass he showed us the envelope that he'd clearly just found in his bag. The other dogs and I went wild as Ashleigh set me on the floor and rushed for the hallway.

So too did Obi and Indi. It didn't matter that the envelope was clearly printed with the show's title underneath the address window. The postman had already made his official delivery. As far as the collies were concerned, the amnesty was over. Despite their ferocious barking, he bravely headed for the door to meet Ashleigh and hand over the letter.

'Really, I think you should let him off this once,' I said to them, but to no avail.

As the postman sprinted back towards the gate with Obi and Indi in hot pursuit, the house was filled with a piercing shriek. It took a moment to realise it had come from Ashleigh, and it was one of surprise and sheer delight.

I turned to my mum, and saw tears of joy in her eyes.

'We did it,' I yelped, as Ashleigh rushed back into the room and into Penny's embrace. 'We're on our way to the auditions!'

Christmas wasn't cancelled that year. Instead, it was dominated by a sense of tension and excitement that even Santa's overnight visit couldn't match. Still, we tried to make things as normal as possible. It was tough, but everyone had a great time. Us dogs exchanged our traditional gifts of Secret Santa sticks we had brought back from walks throughout the year and buried in the garden. Meanwhile Handsome Brad sulked because the pilchard tin we'd retrieved from the bin for him turned out to have been washed up. And we all enjoyed the show put on by Smidgit and the guinea pigs. We thought a line dancing Nativity would be impossible to pull off, but it turned out to be a sensitive and uplifting display. Brad was unusually lost for words and even Shredder calmed down a little bit during the performance. As for Ashleigh, she was thrilled by the gift that Penny and Grandma had worked hard to make for her.

'Check it out, Pudsey,' she said, when we headed for the warmth of the house once more. 'What do you think?'

I stopped in my tracks, as did Indi, Obi and my mum. Only Handsome Brad kept moving, using us for cover to slip inside the house. Ashleigh didn't see him. Instead, having struck a pose, she was waiting for our reaction.

'Is this back in fashion again?' said Obi under his breath. 'It's been out for, what? Two hundred thousand years?'

'It's primitive chic,' Indi suggested, trying to sound like she knew what she was talking about. 'Proper old school.'

I grinned and barked my enthusiasm.

'It's a Stone Age outfit for the show,' I said, and jumped into Ashleigh's arms. 'For our *Flintstones* routine.'

Mum looked on and nodded appreciatively. Ashleigh looked thrilled. She was wearing a little dress made from fake leopard skin, with matching boots and a head-band.

'She looks like a million dollars in the making,' said my mum. 'You both do.'

The New Year united the household in one thing: sheer terror. All of a sudden, the date of the audition was so close it was tempting to chase after it. We had been instructed that the event would take place in Cardiff. Immediately, I began to worry about where I'd left my passport and if I had the correct vaccine shots to cross the border from England into Wales, but my mum assured me that I would be fine.

'You don't need a passport to get into Wales,' she said confidently. 'Nor do you need extra shots. English and Welsh dogs are no different from one another. It's the dragons you need to watch out for.'

With Penny working on the travel arrangements,

Ashleigh and I rehearsed at every available opportunity. We worked hard, but both found it hard to relax.

The collies didn't help. Instead of offering us support, Obi and Indi expressed all the nerves and jitters that I was going through.

'Once you're sure there aren't any dragons circling, make sure you find a tree before you head into the studio,' said Indi. 'You don't want to step out on stage with a full bladder.'

'Or have an accident,' warned Obi. 'Being incontinent isn't a talent, remember.'

As for Handsome Brad, I deliberately steered clear of him. I didn't want him to disturb the focus I was building. Instead, on the morning we were due to head across to Cardiff, I turned to Smidgit. As a former model, she'd had plenty of experience in performing in front of the camera.

'If you happen to catch Simon Cowell's eye,' she told me, 'don't be first to look away.'

'I see,' I said. Baffled as I was, I bowed to her wisdom.

'If you look away first he'll eat you alive. Holding his gaze will earn his respect. Above all, Pudsey, enjoy it! Even if you get no further than the auditions, you'll remember the experience for the rest of your life.'

'Thanks,' I said, repeating this to myself many times over as the other guinea pigs stepped up to wish me luck. When Ashleigh called my name from the back door, I realised this was it.

'You won't be alone,' said Smidgit. 'We'll be with you in spirit.'

I turned and trotted back towards the house. On the way, I caught sight of Handsome Brad on the fence.

'It isn't too late to change your mind, you know?' He flicked his tail one way and then the other as if swatting at a fly. 'I'm just thinking of your dignity.'

'If I backed out now,' I told him, 'I'd never forgive myself.'

'One way or the other,' said the cat with a shrug, 'this is going to end in tears.'

Ashleigh, wearing a warm coat over her outfit, was waiting with Grandma and Penny. I could hear a car engine idling behind the yard gate. Rather than do the driving herself, Penny had struck a deal with a local taxi company. She wanted to sit in the back with us and focus on keeping me calm. Looking at some of the others, I wondered whether she was paying attention to the wrong pet. My mum and the collies paced up and down restlessly, Obi and Indi looking as if they were about to be sick with anxiety.

'Will you relax?' I said, laughing. 'It's bad enough having to deal with my own nerves.'

'I'll take care of these two,' Mum said. 'We'll just be here until Grandma's friend Ethel pops in to feed us and lets us out to stretch our legs.'

'I don't suppose you'll be back until late,' Indi said to me, which seemed to cheer Obi no end.

'So, what this means is we'll be home alone with only an old lady to look in on us?' Obi turned a circle in excitement. 'You know what this means? Let's party on, guys! We're gonna rock this joint!'

I rolled my eyes, smiling despite myself.

'Have fun,' I said, just as the taxi driver sounded his horn to remind us that the meter was ticking.

'Likewise,' said Mum. 'Now go and show the nation what you can do.'

Paws for Thought

My Top Five Smells:
1. Ham Sandwich
2. Simon's aftershave
3. Penny's cooking
4. Any cooking
5. Fox poo

On the way to Wales, Penny, Ashleigh and Grandma discussed exactly what we could expect. Our audition was to take place in the afternoon. We would be in front of a live audience, which sounded scary enough, and the show recorded to go out at a later date. Penny wondered aloud what it would be like to perform in front of the judges – especially Simon Cowell.

'It's going to be tough,' she said. 'He likes dogs, but Pudsey has to shine.'

Just hearing his name brought everything home to me. I had seen the man himself on television, of course. In all the preparation and excitement, however, I hadn't considered what he might make of me.

All of a sudden, I felt like that gangly puppy once again, who'd struggled to put one paw in front of the other. I must've begun to shake at the thought of what lay ahead, because Ashleigh noticed straight away.

'Don't be nervous,' she said, and gave me a cuddle. 'At least, don't be any more nervous than me!'

Once we crossed the toll bridge into Wales, I stopped focusing on the audition for a while. Instead, I kept my eyes peeled for dragons. By the time we came in sight of

Cardiff, though, I began to wonder whether the others had been mistaken. I'd seen no sign of fire-breathing beasts, on land or in the air. On the contrary, it looked like the kind of countryside that a dog would consider paradise. It wasn't just the rolling hillsides but the white fluffy creatures grazing on them. I had never seen so many sheep in my life, and it kept me distracted for ages. The tension in the back of the car only began to thicken as we drove into the city centre though. Penny and Ashleigh stopped chattering and looked out at their surroundings. Finally, the taxi driver leaned over his shoulder and told us that we were nearly there.

He didn't need to spell it out. As soon as I saw the crowds outside the arena where the auditions were taking place, I shrank back inside the back of the cab.

'Nobody told me there'd be a reception,' I whimpered to myself. Again, Ashleigh could tell that I was uncomfortable. This time, however, I was determined to pull myself together. I didn't want her to feel that she needed to take care of me. We were here to look out for each other.

'Are you ready?' asked Penny, as the taxi pulled up. The entrance had been cordoned off with crush barriers, and was filled with acts that had come for a shot at stardom. I had never heard such a din before.

'I'm excited now!' declared Ashleigh. Shaking off her coat, she stepped out with Grandma and smiled at the crowds who had come to watch.

My heart was pounding. This was it. The moment we had been working towards for so long. In a short time from now, we would be dancing on stage. I jumped out after Ashleigh and hopped into her arms. It always felt good. It was like climbing under a duvet. All my worries seemed manageable there. Together, we made our way towards the studio doors, only to be stopped by a roving camera crew and two young men who I recognised straight away. They introduced themselves as Ant and Dec, but their names were so close to basic canine commands I heard just Pant and Beg. When Ashleigh introduced herself and then me, one of them questioned which way round our names should be.

'Pudsey and Ashleigh or Ashleigh and Pudsey?' he asked.

'The first one works for me,' I said under my breath. 'Pudsey and Ashleigh is good.'

'Ashleigh and Pudsey,' said Ashleigh, laughing with the two presenters when they asked her to set it in stone.

I didn't mind being second on the bill. When I thought about it, Ashleigh deserved all the credit for getting us this far. I just knew that Handsome Brad would give me a ribbing about it back home.

Before that, we had the small matter of an audition. On the other side of the revolving doors, once we'd checked in and been given our number, we found ourselves in a crowded lobby. Penny hunted down a good spot, where Ashleigh set about grooming me with a brush. By the time she had finished, there was nothing else left to do but wait. Grandma had brought a packed lunch, including some dog treats, but I wasn't hungry. Nor was

Ashleigh. She was as sunny as ever, but I could sense that she was as keyed up just like me.

Finally, about an hour after we'd arrived, our names were called out.

'Pudsey and Ashleigh?'

'That's Ashleigh and Pudsey,' said Penny to correct the lady with the clipboard who came over to collect us.

'Follow me,' she said, having made the change. 'We're running a little late, but I'm sure you can appreciate how busy we are.'

I only had to look around to see this for myself. The place was packed with hopefuls. Some had made a huge effort with their costumes, others looked as if they had just walked in after a trip to the supermarket. But I didn't want to judge, that wasn't my role. I assumed that every last one of them was here because they'd followed a dream.

The lady with the clipboard led us down a string of corridors and up a flight of stairs. We passed stage crew and several performers making their way back to the lobby. None of them made eye contact with us. Finally, the lady turned and signalled to us to speak quietly, and that's when I realised we had arrived in the wings.

I glanced at Ashleigh. She looked tense, but was still smiling.

'We're just finishing a quick break in the filming,' the lady said. 'You'll be on in no time.'

From the side of the stage, the sound of the audience was incredible. We could hear a wall of excited chatter, and though a curtain blocked our view I could tell that this was going to be big. Members of the production crew were still hurrying about getting everything ready. One man with a headset parted the curtains in order to let a colleague through. That's when I got my first glimpse of the stage and the waiting audience.

I don't know what I was expecting to see, but it came as quite a shock. Maybe it was the lights. Perhaps it was the sheer number of people sitting in tiers up to the roof. All I can remember from that moment was that I had suddenly forgotten one thing. Struck by stage fright, I realised that I couldn't remember the opening move of our routine. Without it, everything else that was supposed to follow just seemed like a jumble in my mind. As a sense of panic rose inside me, a voice on the speaker system announced the return of three individuals who were set to make or break our future in just a matter of moments.

'Ladies and gentlemen, please give a big hand to our judges. Here they come now ... '

Unless I could remember how our routine began, however, I thought I might be better off fleeing from the studio and hoping that Ashleigh would run after me. It would be embarrassing, but nothing could touch the degree of shame we were about to undergo unless that first move came back to me.

'David Walliams, Alesha Dixon and, last but not least ... Simon Cowell!'

18

'The first time I appeared on stage,
it scared me to death.'
Elvis Presley

Have you ever had an out of body experience? Some dogs say it's happened when they found themselves in deep water, or accidentally shut in sheds, and feared their life was about to end. Obi claimed it happened to him when he found out the hard way that chocolate is toxic, and had to have his stomach pumped. I wasn't going to snuff it just then, of course, but I feared that as soon as we stepped out under the stage lights I would die on my backside a million times over.

'Let's go,' said one of the production crew, and gestured for us to head onto the stage.

Ashleigh whispered that she loved me, offered some words of encouragement and then placed me on the floor. I was still desperately trying to remember that crucial first move, but by now my mind was spinning. All I could do was walk on with her and try as hard as possible not to fall over. It was a challenge. As soon as we came in view of the audience, I felt as if my coordination had deserted me completely. You might not appreciate how tough it is under pressure to do something as basic as walking, but let's not forget I have four legs to manage. That's double the multi-tasking demands! I managed to put one front paw ahead of the other, and the same thing at the back. But though I appeared to be moving without a hitch, I felt like I was moving with the grace of a pantomime horse.

When a collective sigh went up from the audience, I wondered if we might at least earn a sympathy vote. Yes, we looked cute, but that wouldn't get us far. Ashleigh stopped in the middle of the stage and faced the front. I did likewise, struggling hard not to pass out on the spot.

'Introduce yourselves, please.'

I heard the voice but didn't match it to the man for a moment. My focus was all over the place, but when I finally got a grip the three figures behind the judging panel came into view. On the left sat David Walliams. He was beaming broadly as if entertaining some delicious secret. Alesha Dixon was beside him, looking like her heart was melting. And to the right was the man awaiting an answer. Simon Cowell didn't seem quite so sold. If anything, he was staring at me as if I'd just trotted muddy paw prints across his stage. I quickly checked, just to reassure myself that I hadn't, and then remembered Smidgit's advice. I levelled my gaze at Simon, and held it there. Ashleigh told him her name, but I only registered her voice when she came to me.

' ... and this is Pudsey.'

'Pudsey.'

With his eyes still locked on me, Simon Cowell repeated my name as if he was trying to get rid of a bad taste from his mouth. I wanted to apologise in advance for wasting his time, but found myself frozen to the spot. Finally, blinking first, Simon turned his attention to Ashleigh. As he grilled her about what we did and where she saw us in a few years' time, I tried in vain to remember that missing move. The only place I could see myself heading just then was home. I wished at that moment we'd never left the kitchen, even though Simon's expression lightened slightly once Ashleigh had answered his questions.

This was largely down to the fact that she had told him I was capable of winning Oscars.

'Um, I wouldn't go that far,' I whispered, but she was fixed on presenting herself as well as possible.

'OK, let's see what you've got,' said Simon. 'Best of luck.'

To the strains of more sighing from the audience, Ashleigh led me towards the far side of the stage. I was searching every last brain cell in my head trying to remember what was expected of me. Each time I drew a blank. When Ashleigh stopped, she directed me to walk around her and then instructed me to place my front paws on her knees. I did this without thinking. We had practised it enough.

Then my nose picked up on what she had tucked away in the palm of one hand. It was a smell that reminded me of all the training we had done together. Instantly, the aromas wafting from that square of ham sandwich summoned up in my mind the move that I was convinced I had forgotten.

As soon as the blare of the big band opened up with the *Flintstones* soundtrack, Ashleigh and I spun into action. I knew exactly what to do and where I had to be next. I barely had to think about it, in fact. Everything locked in place like a chain. I heard gasps from the audience, whistles of admiration and applause, all of which drove me to make sure this performance was the best we had ever put on.

I twirled and jumped and walked on my hind legs. It felt like something I had been doing all my life, but judging by the reaction in the studio nobody had ever seen anything like it before. Once or twice I caught Ashleigh's eye. She was focusing hard, making sure I registered every command, until the final one came to spring into her arms, just as the music ended.

And that's when everything went crazy.

'Good boy!' cried Ashleigh, and squeezed me so hard that it almost felt as if this could still end in tragedy.

Amid the roar of applause, I saw people rise to their feet, and that included the judges. I sat in Ashleigh's arms, panting from the performance, and grinned at what we had achieved. I heard Alesha and David heap praise upon us, but it was Ashleigh's delighted response to it all that meant the most. Then Simon announced that this was the act he had been waiting for, and at that point I must've caught a speck of dust in my eye. You must understand, I wasn't crying. Oh no. Not like humans do. When a dog loses it, we don't reach for the hankies, we look the same as ever. But on the inside, I broke down in sheer relief and happiness.

Then Simon announced that it was time to vote.

'David, yes or no?' he asked, and looked across the panel.

Mr Walliams seemed to be going for a dramatic pause, but took one look at us and crumbled.

'A million per cent, yes!' he declared and thumped the panel.

I glanced up at Ashleigh. She was beaming with pride, seemingly unconcerned by what he'd just said.

'What does that mean?' I asked, and looked back at him grinning at us. 'Do the maths, friend! There's no such thing as a million per cent! Even I know that. It's a hundred per cent, and that's where it ends.'

I wasn't really cross with him. How could I be after such a show of support? When David's enthusiasm was backed up by Alesha, I switched my attention to the man on the end. Simon was no longer looking at me like I'd made a mess of his stage. If anything, he seemed quite pleased to have us there. Clearly the performance had won him over, though I like to think that Smidgit's advice to hold my ground in the staring contest beforehand had helped. But what he had to say next just blew us both away. I don't remember a word, but I'm told he claimed that I was the best dancing dog he'd ever seen. Then he caught my eye again, only this time I saw steel in his gaze.

'My only criticism is this,' he said to finish, which caused the audience to go quiet. 'I would've put Pudsey in a prehistoric outfit as well.'

He was clearly joking, and the comment provoked much laughter from the other judges and the audience. But that didn't stop me growling at him under my breath.

'You can try, pal,' I muttered. 'But you'll be sorry.'

When the laughter fell away, fortunately leaving my pride intact, I found him beaming at me. I grinned back, well aware that there was a very nice man in front of us trapped inside the body of a hardened impresario. Mr Cowell drew breath to address us once more, but I just knew from the twinkle in his eye that this wasn't the end.

'Congratulations, Ashleigh and Pudsey. You're through to the next round!'

19

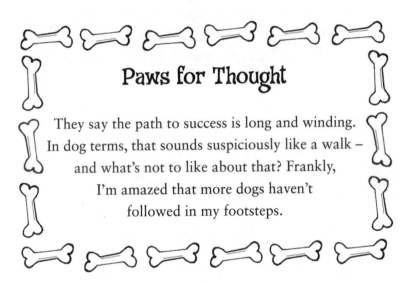

Paws for Thought

They say the path to success is long and winding.
In dog terms, that sounds suspiciously like a walk –
and what's not to like about that? Frankly,
I'm amazed that more dogs haven't
followed in my footsteps.

We were very late home that night. I was bursting to share our good news with everyone, but the dogs were fast asleep. At least my mum was. When Penny flicked on the kitchen light and switched off the radio, Obi and Indi pretended to stir from a deep slumber. As they did so, Penny looked around and frowned.

'This place is in a state,' she said, picking up an empty box of dog treats from the floor. It had been torn open, judging by the shreds of cardboard around it. 'It even smells of cat pee,' she moaned. 'What have you been doing while we were away?'

As she crossed to the bin, Obi climbed out and pretended to yawn.

'You missed quite a party, Pudsey,' he whispered. 'It was still going strong a minute ago. Then we heard the car pull up so naturally everyone made themselves scarce.'

'Everyone?' I asked, as Penny began collecting all our toys, which were supposed to be kept in a box.

'It was a blast,' said Indi. 'Of course, it's Handsome Brad's fault things got out of control. He invited a load of his feline mates around. You know how edgy things can get between cats and dogs.'

'The Persian started it,' Obi pointed out. 'Any cat who begins a debate about who makes a better hunter is just asking for trouble. I think chasing him around the house for half an hour proved my point.'

'The fact that you didn't catch him kind of proved his,' Indi said to counter.

By now, my mum was out of her bed and stretching. 'The whole evening was too rowdy for my old bones,' she said, and padded across to sniff me. 'Do I detect the smell of victory?' she asked, and stepped back to look at me.

Just then Ashleigh appeared at the door. She had just helped Grandma into the spare room, where she was staying the night.

'We made it!' she announced to the collies and my mum. 'Pudsey and I are through!'

Obi looked at me.

'You're kidding?'

I shook my head.

'You can watch it all on television this Saturday night.'

Obi turned to Indi.

'Did you hear that? Oh, man. I've got to see Brad's face when he learns about this. Do we tell him now, or wait until he watches the show for himself?'

'Now that would just be cruel,' said Indi, and then glanced at every one of us, as a smile began to cross her face. 'Nobody say a word, understood?'

I found it very difficult to contain my news. Whenever Brad showed up, us dogs either made out we were fast asleep or simply stayed out of his way. As it was so early in the year, his interest quickly turned to finding a radiator, so we managed to keep my secret safe.

'Brad thinks you earned three "no's" from the judges,' said Smidgit, who I had told at the earliest opportunity. 'He reckons you're avoiding him because you're too ashamed to admit he was right all along.'

I smiled at this, but part of me felt bad about stringing him along.

'Should I just tell him the truth?' I asked her.

Smidgit considered this for a moment. She turned to face the other guinea pigs. All of them shook their heads.

'Make him wait,' she said. 'I'd love to see the moment when he finds out.'

'It's a shame you can't join us to watch the show,' I said.

'Well, maybe I will,' she replied mysteriously, before retiring to her sleeping quarters.

The guinea pigs were Penny's passion in life. She took great care of them all, and groomed them regularly. Smidgit in particular required frequent attention. Her coat needed brushing all the time. So, at tea time on the Saturday that the show went out, when Penny popped down to feed them and found her looking like she'd dragged herself through a hedge backwards, Smidgit was promptly transported into the front room for a beauty session in front of the TV. Everyone was gathered there, including Ashleigh and Grandma. With the dogs

Indi is a dangerous
dog to go walking
with when canals
are involved. Just
ask Obi.

The first rule of Walking Club? You do not talk
about Walking Club.

I actually became rather good at agilit

In fact, I even made it Olympic standard! Sadly my 'Hot Dog' move - the canine equivalent of the Mobot or Lightning Bolt - failed to take the nation by storm.

imitive chic. Ashleigh in her
wesome *Flintstones* costume. And
e? Perfectly happy in my birthday
it, thank you very much.

Arriving in London for the
semi-finals, with Ashleigh and
Penny. I'm walking fast to avoid
the pigeons.

A photocall with the other semi-finalists. Sadly I couldn't
tuck into the croissants due to my strict pre-dance diet.

Backstage at the semis, and still spaced out after a monumental stress-sleep.

In a routine packed with challenging moves, this one was one of the toughest. Ashleigh calls it the hoop, I call it the psychopathic crocodile . . .

One *seriously* dramatic entrance for the final.

O.M.G! Somewhere in the middle of all that ticker tape is one very happy dog and his amazing friend (that's Ashleigh, not Pant or Beg).

Heading back to the hotel. I'm being carried because I'm tired, **not** because I've been enjoying the champagne, before any journalists sniff an exposé.

Helping to put away the vacuum cleaner after the rest of the guys trashed the lounge during the final.

PUDSEY   ASHLEIGH

So, where do we go from here . . . ?

I'll give you a clue . . .

on the hearth in front of the fire, there was only one thing missing.

'Where's Handsome Brad?' I asked as the opening credits to *Britain's Got Talent* rolled.

'I'm here,' came his reply. 'I wouldn't miss this for the world.'

I looked around, but saw no sign of him. It was Mum who nodded towards the coffee table. I peered underneath, and saw him there facing the screen.

'Listen, Brad,' I said, uncomfortable about what he was about to see. 'There's something you should know.' Every animal looked in my direction, silently urging me to keep quiet.

'What's the problem?' asked the cat. 'If you want permission to sit this one out I understand. I wouldn't like to watch myself become a national laughing stock.'

'Pudsey just wanted to be sure you're prepared,' squeaked Smidgit. Penny was carefully combing through her coat, but like everyone else her attention was fixed on the screen.

'Oh, I'm ready,' purred Brad. 'I've been looking forward to this all week!'

It was strange to see Ashleigh and me on the television. They say it puts on ten pounds. That didn't apply to Ashleigh, who was dazzling, but I looked like I'd put away one too many crispy pig's ears. Frankly, I didn't think I looked like a dog that was capable of anything much, so when our turn came under the stage lights it was a thrill to hear the audience response all over again.

'I'm so proud of you,' my mum whispered, as the

camera cut from our dance to the growing look of surprise and delight on the judges' faces.

'Pudsey was perfect!' Ashleigh told her mother. 'It was as if he knew this was our big moment.'

'Oh, I knew,' I whispered to Obi and Indi.

As Ashleigh, Penny and Grandma relived what had gone through their minds at the time, I watched Handsome Brad's grin begin to weaken. When our performance came to an end, he even shot me an uneasy look.

'Here we go,' he said all the same. 'This show is about people not pets. Prepare to crash and burn!'

Knowing what would follow, it seemed to me that the ginger tom might as well have been talking to himself. As each judge gave their verdict, Brad's expression switched from surprise to shock and disbelief. Then he turned to me looking completely betrayed.

'I'm sorry,' I said. 'We should've told you.'

Despite the scenes of jubilation on the screen, Brad found every pet looking at him.

'Your face!' joked Obi.

'Classic,' Indi agreed, and chuckled along with Mum.

I glanced at Smidgit. She too seemed to be relishing the moment. Perhaps it was because they'd lived under his shadow for so long. Just then I wished I'd gone with my instincts and found a quiet time to tell Brad we had made it. Judging by the way that he was clearly seething, I realised it was far too late for that.

'Ever since Pudsey showed up here this place hasn't been the same,' he snarled under the sound of the television. 'It's like that prancing pooch has become more important than your pack leader – and that's something you could live to regret!'

Unaware of this exchange, let alone the presence of a cat in the house, Ashleigh and Grandma were up on their feet and hugging once again. Seizing his opportunity, and leaving us with a glare, Handsome Brad slipped from the room before anyone could stop him.

20

'I just put my feet on the ground and
move them around.'
Fred Astaire

I had no time to feel bad about our treatment of the ginger tom. Ashleigh and I were through to the semi-final rounds! Instead of months to train for our audition, we had just weeks to prepare a new performance. It meant we needed another song and dance routine, and fast.

Naturally, the pets made plenty of suggestions, from the interesting to the frankly bizarre. Obi's idea that we could work out to the theme tune to *Jaws* was dismissed by Indi and my mum as being too upsetting for young viewers, while Smidgit wondered out loud whether we should both put on blue face paint and recreate a scene from *Avatar*.

'Look, I appreciate the support,' I told them. 'But I'd rather go for a walk in a thunderstorm.'

In the end, Ashleigh and Penny decided we should dance in tribute to another talented dog, and opted for the theme tune to *The Artist*. As soon as that was settled, we spent every moment outside school hours getting ready all over again. It was both exciting and exhausting, going to bed late and rising before everyone else so that we could squeeze in a session at the agility centre.

Several days into our training, having been let into the garden by Penny at the break of dawn, I came across Handsome Brad. It was the first time I had seen him since he'd left the front room in a fury after our televised performance.

'You know what sunrise says to a cat?' he asked, sounding far calmer now. 'Bed time. That's what it says. After a hard night's prowling, first light means it's time to turn in.'

Brad was sitting on the fence behind the guinea pig run. Smidgit and the others were sound asleep. I could hear them snoring in the shed. Brad was bathed in the day's first horizontal bars of light. I tipped my back leg against the bush to give it its daily watering down, and then addressed him directly.

'Brad, I want to apologise for embarrassing you.'

'It's forgotten,' he said, and batted it away with one paw. 'If people want to applaud a dog that can stand on its hind legs that's their problem, not mine.'

'Why is it a problem?' I asked, sounding puzzled.

Brad was still facing the sun with his eyes closed, enjoying the early heat.

'After your performance,' he said, 'I should imagine every owner in the land is busy training his dog to walk. It's cute. It's funny. It's also asking for trouble. Because when all dogs learn to rise up like you can that's an evolutionary step mankind might find kind of threatening. It's how wars begin, Pudsey. Dogs could find themselves wiped from the face of the planet because you dared to dance to *The Flintstones*.'

I listened to his theory without even blinking.

'I'd never thought about it like that,' I said, feeling very concerned all of a sudden about what I might have started.

Handsome Brad opened his eyes and looked down at me. A moment later, a big grin spread across his face.

'I'm messing with you,' he said. 'There aren't many dogs like you, Pudsey. I dare say you're one of a kind.'

'Thanks,' I said. It was too early in the morning to be as sharp as Brad, but I felt relief all the same. 'So, I was thinking. Can we start all over again?'

Brad looked me up and down for a moment.

'I hear you've been training hard for the semi-finals,' he said eventually. 'I'm proud of you pushing on like that.'

'You are?' I was surprised at how forgiving Brad was being with me. It was good to hear. 'Ashleigh and I have got a great routine worked out.'

'I look forward to seeing it,' said Brad. 'How high do you have to jump this time?'

'Oh, really high,' I said, delighted that the cat was showing such an interest. 'Halfway through, Ashleigh makes a loop with her arms and I have to take a run up to jump through. So far it hasn't gone wrong,' I finished, and tapped the side of my head. 'Touch wood.'

Brad nodded, looking suitably impressed.

'Reckon you could clear this fence?' he asked.

At first, I wasn't clear I had heard him correctly.

'I'm sure,' I said eventually, 'but I don't want to upset Shredder.'

'The bulldog?' Handsome Brad glanced over his shoulder. 'That lazy mutt doesn't wake up for ages.'

I pricked my ears. It was unusual to be having a conversation like this without Shredder leaping up and down behind Brad.

'It's certainly quiet,' I agreed.

'So go for it,' said Brad, and padded along the fence as if to make way for me. 'Unless it's too high, of course.'

It would take quite a leap, I thought to myself, but I figured I could scramble over. I glanced at Brad nervously.

'Are you sure about this?'

'Would I play tricks on you?' Brad glanced into the garden once more, and returned his gaze to me. 'I guess it comes down to trust.'

I sighed to myself, feeling caught. I was sure that I could scale the fence. It was something I did regularly on agility courses. But this time I wasn't doing it to prove anything to myself. It was Brad who was asking me to believe in him.

'OK,' I said hesitantly, 'but I'll need a run up.'

'Show me what you can do, Pudsey,' he said calmly.

I trotted back across the garden and turned. In my mind I could hear Ashleigh issuing commands and encouragement. It was all I needed as I raced towards the fence, raising my paws at the same time to connect with it and then push myself over the top.

I landed effortlessly, and then took a breath. Sure enough, Shredder wasn't in the garden. He was watching me from the kitchen. I could see him clearly, because the back door was wide open.

'Oh,' I said, and retreated a step. All of a sudden, I felt completely trapped. 'Now be a good doggie and we'll pretend this never happened.'

I glanced back at Brad, who was watching with interest.

'Oops,' he said.

If Shredder had just finished wolfing down his breakfast, he clearly still had an appetite for violence, bad language and bloodshed, judging by the way he came tearing out of the house towards me. With his head down, charging at full tilt, he truly put the bull into bulldog.

'All right, time to go!' I turned around and sprinted as fast as my legs would carry me. Unfortunately, it wasn't fast enough. My jump lacked the grace of the previous one and I struggled to reach the top of the fence with my front paws. Even Brad looked alarmed when I fell back down and prepared in desperation for a second attempt.

'Quick, Pudsey!' he cried, turning on the fence now. 'Come on, buddy. Get out of there!'

By now, Shredder was tearing across the garden, turning the air blue with all manner of curses and threats about what he would do with me. I didn't want to hang around to see if he was joking, and ran for the fence again. This time, I got my front paws onto the top, but struggled for grip with my hind legs. I could hear the guinea pigs rushing from the shed, roused by all the noise, and Smidgit shrieking at them to try to distract the dog through the knotholes.

'Pudsey's life depends on it!' she yelled, as the dog below me leapt for my tail. He fell away with a bunch of hairs between his teeth, which was enough for me to muster one last effort. With a yelp, I hauled myself out of danger and tumbled back into our garden.

'Are you hurt?' Brad dropped down beside me. He sounded panic-stricken. 'Say something, Pudsey! Anything! A sign that you're still with us!'

'I'm a little winded,' I croaked, as Shredder could be heard snarling and frothing at the mouth on the other side of the fence.

'It was just a joke that went wrong!' Brad reasoned as I picked myself up and shook myself down. 'It was only supposed to give you a scare,' he added, and hung his head. 'I knew that back door was open. I just didn't think Shredder could move so fast.'

'Pudsey could've been killed back then!' Smidgit was at the wire to her run, yelling furiously at the cat. 'How could you do that? And why?'

Brad looked thoroughly shamefaced.

'I'm sorry,' he said, turning back to me. 'I guess I'm just jealous of what you've achieved, Pudsey. But you didn't deserve that. Soon as I thought you might be hurt, I realised what I'd done was wrong.'

'I'm all right,' I said and checked my tail. 'It's over now.'

I faced back to Brad, and found him looking at me intently.

'You asked if we could make a fresh start,' he said, and then cleared his throat of a fur ball. 'I'd like that.'

Just then, the sound of the back door opening was met by squeaking and squealing from the guinea pigs. Once Penny had fed them breakfast, it would be time for us to hop into her car and head to the agility centre. Brad was about to make himself scarce. Before he did so, however, I caught his eye once more.

'I told you I could jump that fence,' I said with a wink, and padded off to see if Ashleigh was ready.

21

Paws for Thought

If there's one aspect of our personalities that gives us more of a bad rap than any other, it's our loyalty. We're all or nothing, and once you've earned it you can tell us anything and we'll believe you! If Ashleigh says she's popping out for five minutes and doesn't return for an hour, you won't find me scowling at the door and pointing at the clock. I'm just delighted to see her again! You don't get that with other animals, particularly cats …

Like the other dogs, I was doubtful that Brad had genuinely seen the light. According to Obi and Indi, cats are closely related to leopards and everyone knows they can't change their spots. Like my mum, however, I was prepared to give him a chance. To my delight, throughout the build-up to the semi-finals, the ginger tom offered me extra coaching in the finer points of feline acrobatics.

'Cats are all about balance and poise,' he told me. 'That's where our confidence comes from, and it shows. You need to believe in yourself, Pudsey. Don't just go through the moves. Own them!'

Handsome Brad was a hard taskmaster. Several times he made me walk along the fence at the bottom of the garden. With Shredder gnashing and snapping on one side, and the guinea pigs rooting for me on the other, I found that by tuning out from both sides and lifting my tail high I could get across in one piece. When I introduced the technique to the performance that Ashleigh and I had strung together, even she noticed that I had raised my game.

'Pudsey's showing real grace at the moment,' she told Penny. 'I can't think where it's coming from.' I chose to ignore the implication that I wasn't a natural (mainly because it was true).

Naturally, Handsome Brad took all the credit, but that was fine by me. Along with the dogs and the guinea pigs, he had pushed me just like Ashleigh, but in ways I never thought possible. It meant that when the time arrived for us to set off for London, to perform in front of the judges for a second time, I couldn't have been better prepared. Instead of being riddled with nerves, as I had been the first time round, I was actually looking forward to stepping out on stage.

'Looking good,' said Brad as we prepared to leave. 'Bring out your inner cat on the night, and you'll be sure to dazzle them.'

Penny, Ashleigh and Grandma were loading bags into the taxi. Once again, Ashleigh had put together a brilliant outfit that this time made her look like a silver-screen star-let. I sat at the yard gate with the other dogs, while the ginger tom was perched on the woodshed roof overlooking us all.

'Pudsey's a dog,' Obi reminded him. 'He doesn't have an inner cat.'

'If he did,' said Indi, 'it would be hell in there.'

I glanced up at Brad and chuckled.

'Brad's taught me a thing or two,' I said to back him up. 'But I've no interest in rodents or moving somewhere warmer, even when they turn off the radiators.'

'Nothing wrong with a little self-interest,' said Brad from up above, as if addressing us from a pulpit. 'Good luck, Pudsey. Look forward to hearing how you get on.'

I tipped my head in surprise.

'The semi-final is live on television tonight,' I said to

remind him. 'Won't you be watching it with everyone else?'

'That depends.' Handsome Brad sampled the air with his head tipped back. 'I should imagine some of the guys will be round again. Plus I'll have to see if there's anything on the other side.'

I glanced at the collies, unsure if he was joking. That's the thing about cats. You can never tell when they're playing you for a fool.

The sound of the boot of the taxi shutting told me we were ready to go.

'Wish us luck,' I said to Mum, though I knew she didn't need to put it into words. She had supported me from the start, as had Obi and Indi.

'You can count on us,' said Indi. 'We'll be rooting for you.'

'Even if Brad invites the boys round again,' Obi chipped in, 'the party stops when you perform!'

I had it on good authority from my mum that there were no dragons in London. Apparently they had been driven out long ago by the pigeons.

Just one mention of those birds had given me flashbacks to the time I'd spent wandering the streets, but I wasn't going to let that ruin my day. In fact, I stayed calm and cool during the journey. At least I did until we reached London. Once we were off the motorway, Ashleigh wound down the rear window so that I could get some fresh air. I couldn't resist popping my head out to feel the wind on my face. As we drove past the Houses of Parliament and then Westminster Abbey, I found myself barking with excitement. I must admit I tried to bite the double decker buses as they passed, but Penny soon put a stop to that. We weren't here to upset the traffic.

As for the pigeons, I was shocked at how many there were. I wasn't surprised that they had taken out the dragons, though I saw many bearing battle scars. These guys looked meaner than the flock that had tried to shake me down. Some of them looked like they were hiding bird-sized baseball bats under their wings. Still, it didn't stop me from barking at them too, because by then we were well on our way to our destination. There, in a few hours' time, our future would be decided one way or the other.

If the size of the venue for the auditions had surprised me, this one took my breath away. It was huge, as were the crowds outside. Most surprisingly of all, some people seemed to know my name, including a lot of photographers.

'Pudsey! Over here! Ashleigh, Pudsey ...'

I jumped into Ashleigh's arms to have our picture taken, before Penny hurried us in. This time, the lobby wasn't packed with hopefuls and looking like an airport check-in. As one of only a handful of acts due to perform later that evening, we were greeted personally by a member of the production staff, who took us straight up to a dressing room.

'I can't believe it,' whispered Ashleigh. 'This is proper show business!'

I wondered what we might find once we arrived. Ashleigh and Penny joked about grapes and a bowl of Smarties with all the red ones removed. I just held out hope for a bowl of water. It was important that I didn't eat too much. When it came to hitting the stage, my nose needed to be locked onto the aroma of the ham sandwich square that Ashleigh wafted with such precision. As it turned out, we didn't have time to settle in. I had only just sniffed around the edges of the room when a lady from make-up arrived.

'OK, who's first?' she asked, looking between Ashleigh and me.

'Ah, dogs don't do make-up,' I pointed out quietly, but Penny was laughing so hard that nobody heard. No way was I going to appear on television wearing blusher, lipstick and eyeliner, and so I hid behind Ashleigh to spell that out.

Half an hour later, we were ready to rehearse. This time, we didn't just step onto an empty stage. We had backing dancers and a light show that dazzled me. Watching everyone at work, I felt like the only amateur on set. How those sure-footed guys behind us knew how to hit their marks without the aid of a ham sandwich I'll never know. Still, I was impressed, and determined to do well. It was weird, though, to dance to an empty theatre, even if some of the crew stopped to watch. One or two even applauded, but I didn't think we had earned it. Every time

I got up on my hind legs, I wobbled a little too much. It was frustrating for me because Ashleigh was on fire with her performance and I didn't want to let her down. I decided there was only one thing for it.

When the going gets tough for a dog, the best thing that the dog can do is get some sleep.

Curled up under the dressing-room mirror, I fell into a deep slumber. Let me tell you, being nervous is knackering! Still, at least it meant that when I surfaced the waiting was over. In fact, I found there was no time left for any lingering doubts at all.

'Come on, Pudsey!' said Ashleigh from the door. 'We're on!'

She had left me to sleep for as long as possible. As soon as I followed her into the corridor, a roar of applause marked the end of the performance of the act before us. I felt rested, but a little disorientated. I was also well aware that I needed to wake up fast. We joined Penny and Grandma in the wings. Grandma was peering out at the judging panel.

'David's looking handsome today,' she whispered, her eyes fixed on him. 'I love him.'

'Grandma,' hissed Penny. 'Not now. Not ever, in fact!'

'Sorry.'

This time, Pant and Beg were out on stage. They were wearing smart suits and big smiles as they talked to the judges. It was good to see that Amanda Holden had joined Simon, David and Alesha on the panel. Obi had a soft spot for Amanda. And Handsome Brad liked Alesha, even if he refused to admit it. I was just thinking about the pets back home when the boys introduced the next act.

'That's us,' I said with a gasp, on hearing our names.

'Hurry,' whispered Ashleigh. 'We need to take our places!'

As the stage lights dimmed, a group of grinning male dancers in tuxedoes lined up at the front of the stage. Each was clutching a clapperboard, as if preparing to start shooting a movie scene. In a dazzling white dress that sparkled with sequins, Ashleigh certainly looked like a star – I just hoped that I could help make her soar. Leading me out behind the dancers, Ashleigh patted my head and showed me the all-important sandwich.

'I'm good to go,' I told her, as the very first sequence materialised in my mind. 'Bring it on, baby!'

That evening, live on air, we didn't just dance for the judges and the audience. We performed for the nation. And yet the strangest thing is that when the spotlight fell upon us we could've been dancing alone. I only had eyes for Ashleigh, and she looked the same way about me. My one conscious thought throughout was to move with the grace of a cat, but apart from that I just relished the moment. It felt as if we were in a dream world, and I only came back to reality when the stage lights went up again to wild applause.

The judges were on their feet. The first thing I did was find Simon Cowell's gaze and hold it steady. Still clapping, he winked at me and then turned to grin at his fellow judges. Soaking up the atmosphere, Ashleigh chose that moment to shower me with kisses. Despite finding myself covered in her lipstick, I kept on looking at Simon, waiting for him to face back to me, and when he did so I knew that he was about to make us the happiest dancing dog act in the world.

22

Look into my eyes, Mr Cowell …

The next morning, back at home, I took some convincing from the others that it hadn't just been a dream.

'You blew us all away!' Obi was pacing excitedly around the kitchen, even though we were some minutes away from breakfast. 'Everyone watched you. Even Brad and his gang.'

'So, his friends came round after all,' I said. I didn't like to ask about the damage this time around.

Indi was still sprawled across her pillow. She could clearly read my mind.

'We tried our best to clear up the mess,' she told me. 'The trouble with those cats is they have no respect for other people's houses. They just breeze in and act like they own the place.'

'Anyway,' my mum said, moving the subject along. 'You and Ashleigh made us so proud last night. Can you believe it? The final!'

As she spoke, a knock at the front door prompted us all to surge into the hall. A moment later, as we barked and bayed at the figure on the other side of the frosted glass, Penny beat a path between us and ordered us to settle down. Once we were quiet she opened the door, only for a foot to appear on the threshold.

'We're from the press,' said a man with a camera strung

around his neck. Penny barely had time to draw breath before he thrust a card in her face. Behind him, several more photographers strained to get a view. One even took a picture, just as Ashleigh appeared at the foot of the stairs, blinding us all when the flash went off. 'Can we get a shot?' he asked, a little belatedly.

If I had to put my paw on it, this was the moment our lives began to change. Overnight, through the eyes of the media we had become rising stars. Penny's mobile phone didn't stop ringing. The only reason the house phone stayed quiet is because Mum had become fed up with it waking her up all morning and nosed it off the hook. It was exciting. A real thrill. At the same time, it was pretty tiring. We had made it through to the last show, despite my misgivings, and now Ashleigh and I had even less time to prepare a fresh routine. We needed it to soar over the competition, only now we couldn't step outside to rehearse without being dazzled by photographers' flashbulbs.

Fortunately, the collies stepped up to provide us with the peace and quiet we needed.

'No need to worry about the paps any more,' Obi assured me one morning. 'Indi and I have got the side gates covered. And I think we all know Shredder won't be too accommodating if a photographer tries to sneak a shot from round the back.'

'The only person with permission to reach the front

door is the postman,' Indi added. 'He has precisely ten seconds to make it to the house and back. Otherwise he forfeits the seat of his trousers. Again.'

It was a kind gesture – though maybe not for the postman – and it freed us up to prepare a final routine. This time, when Ashleigh suggested the theme tune to *Mission Impossible*, everyone agreed it was absolutely perfect. The tune was big, bold, ambitious and fast-moving. Just like me, in fact. For days on end we worked out the best way to push our dancing skills to the maximum. Eventually, Ashleigh came up with an idea.

'You're going to run across the judges' table,' she told me one afternoon. 'It'll be like an elevated walkway at the agility centre – only if you slip you'll end up in a very expensive lap.'

'And a lawsuit,' Indi added, unhelpfully.

I understood what was expected of me. Whenever Ashleigh was at school I'd continue to practise with the help of my friends. Home alone, we'd push out the sofa so I could dash along the back of it. Obi, Indi and my mum would sit on the cushions facing me and pretend to be the judges.

'Can I just stop you there,' said Obi on one occasion, doing his best Simon Cowell impression. 'A dancing dog's all very well, but he's nothing without an entourage. I vote for Pudsey so long as he doesn't forget his friends when he's on the VIP list at Chinawhite.'

'I won't do that,' I told him, laughing at the same time. 'Everyone's been so supportive.'

When I said this, I even had Brad in mind. It went

without saying that Smidgit and the guinea pigs were behind me every step of the way, but as the all-important Saturday approached it was the ginger tom who did something for me that I'll never forget.

'You know what?' the cat said to me, sidling up after I had finished practising with Ashleigh one afternoon. 'I might just watch the final.'

'That would mean a great deal,' I told him.

'I'm not promising,' he said. 'If *Top Cat*'s on one of the cable channels then I'll tape it and watch you later.'

'Right,' I said, aware of the playful glint in his eye. 'Well, your advice to me has been brilliant. As a dog, I'm never going to admit to unleashing my inner feline, but it's worked wonders so far.'

'If I was a dog I'd want to keep that under wraps, too,' said Brad, nodding. 'But I'm glad it's worked out. I've never seen Ashleigh look so happy.'

The cat meant well when he said this, but it also troubled me.

'I'm not so sure that happiness is going to last,' I told him. 'Have you seen the competition we're up against in the final? Only Boys Aloud? Jonathan and Charlotte? Ryan O'Shaughnessy? Some of those acts are terrific. We've done brilliantly to get this far, but I can't help thinking our luck's about to run out.'

'Then you've done the right thing by talking to me.' Brad paced full circle around me. I heard him chewing at something, followed by a popping sound. When he came back into my line of sight, he had something sparkling in his teeth, which he spat in front of me. 'Take this,' he said.

'What is it?' I asked, inspecting the offering on the grass. I was looking at a clear plastic stud with a clasp beside it.

'A charm,' said Brad, as if I should've known that for myself. 'A lucky one.'

I looked up at the cat. He turned his head to show me one side of his collar. I hadn't paid it any attention before, but now I saw that it was decorated all the way around with identical studs. Some were missing, one of which I figured he'd just managed to pull away for me.

'How did you manage that?' I asked. I had never seen my own collar. I always thought it was physically impossible for an animal to do that, in the same way that a human will never see their own shoulder blades.

'I'm a cat,' said Brad. 'Cats can do a lot of things that would blow your tiny canine mind. Now stop asking questions and just accept it.'

'But it looks valuable,' I said, inspecting the charm once more.

'I still have a couple left,' Brad told me with a shrug. 'Let's face it, us cats start out in the world with nine. You could say luck is on our side.'

It took a moment for me to realise what this represented. I raised my eyes back to the cat, shocked by the gesture.

'This is one of your nine lives?' I asked. 'Brad, it's so kind, but I can't accept it.'

'I'm not that generous,' he told me, 'it's just a loan. To help you feel more confident. I'll want it back after the final.'

I studied the charm once more. I would take anything

that helped me feel positive. Performing tricks wasn't all about technical skill. A lot of it was in the mind, and the sheer belief that I could pull it off.

'You sound very sure that I won't need to use it,' I said.

Handsome Brad flashed a grin at me. 'Pudsey, you haven't put a paw wrong yet. I have no doubt you'll do just fine, but take it anyway. Before I get offended.'

I didn't tell the other dogs what the cat had done for me. As a gesture, it was so special I felt it was something that only Brad and I should know about. For the last few days before we travelled back to London, I hid his lucky charm under my basket. I wanted to take it with me, but I didn't know how. The solution only came to me during my last practice with Ashleigh. She was trying out her new outfit to make sure that it fitted properly. Brad would've approved of her catsuit, but since lending me the charm I hadn't seen head nor tail of him. There was no way I would be zipping myself into costume as Simon Cowell had suggested, but it struck me all of a sudden that there was one thing I could wear.

'Where are you off to?' asked Ashleigh, just as we completed the final sequence in the performance. I pretended not to hear her, and hurried into the house. Returning with the charm and the clasp between my teeth, I dropped both at her feet just as Brad had done for me. Then I sat down, looked up at her expectantly and wagged my tail. Ashleigh collected the stud between two fingers and inspected it in the light. 'It's pretty,' she said, and faced me once more.

I didn't have to spell out what I wanted her to do. Ashleigh and I had worked so closely for years that it almost felt as if she could read my mind. My mum wandered out just then, intrigued by what I was up to.

'It's just a thing,' I told her, tilting my head for Ashleigh. 'Don't ask who gave it to me.'

The stud passed effortlessly through my collar. Ashleigh fitted the clasp and nodded appreciatively.

'Wherever that came from,' she said, and tickled me behind the ear, 'let's hope it brings us luck!'

I turned to show my mum. She narrowed her eyes.

'I've seen that somewhere before,' she said, looking quietly impressed and at the same time amused. 'So, Handsome Brad has a heart after all.'

'He just wants the best for us,' I told her.

'We all do, Pudsey,' she replied. 'No matter what this weekend has in store.'

23

'Your mission, should you choose to accept it ...'
Mission Impossible

Much to the delight of the collie dogs, our trip to London this time involved an overnight stay. Due to all the media interest in the finalists, Ashleigh, Penny, Grandma and I would be visiting the capital not for one day but two.

'So, you're leaving us in the company of Brad and his friends for forty-eight hours?' Obi asked, just to make sure. 'You do know it's going to be messy here, right?'

'We're lucky the cat doesn't have a Facebook account,' said Indi, nodding in agreement. 'He'd post an open party invitation and we'd end up with hordes of cats in the house.'

'We'll probably be overrun anyway,' Mum said with a sigh. 'Cats are well connected even without social media. They all know each other in the neighbourhood.'

I didn't like to think about what the dogs would get up to while we were away. Grandma's friend, Ethel, would be popping in again to feed and walk them, but they'd still have plenty of time on their hands to make mayhem. Still, it was important that I focused on just one thing, and that was our performance. Ashleigh was in a similar frame of mind. We were both subdued on the journey down. Until, that is, we arrived at the hotel that the show had organised for us.

'OK, everyone mind your manners and be sure to wipe

your feet when we step inside,' said Penny in amazement. 'I've never seen anything so posh in all my life!'

Before Ashleigh or Grandma could reply, the hotel doorman was striding towards the taxi in order to help us out. Even the pavement was red carpeted, I realised, hopping out behind Ashleigh. I really needed a pee after such a long journey, but this was no place to be cocking my leg.

As we discovered inside, it turned out to be no place for a dog at all.

'Can I stop you there,' said a man behind the desk in a heavy French accent. We'd barely passed through the double doors before he'd risen to his feet and shown me his palm. 'Dogs are not to be permitted in *l'hôtel.*'

'But it's all been arranged,' said Penny, as Ashleigh and Grandma looked anxiously at one another.

'Rules are rules,' he said and folded his arms. 'You can stay, but not ze dog.'

A low growl built in the back of my throat. The man looked at me disapprovingly. Across the lobby, I recognised one of the acts we were up against waiting for the lift doors to open. It was good enough for them, I thought, but clearly not for me.

'OK, we're leaving,' said Penny, and gestured for everyone to turn around. 'We'll find somewhere a little more pet friendly.'

I was last through the revolving doors. I didn't look back, though I did pause to relieve myself against the solid oak frame and then scarpered as the man gave chase.

It took a while to find somewhere to stay that would

have me. The place we finally booked into was cheap, basic – and to be honest it was just what I needed. Everyone was really friendly and I didn't have to worry about shedding hair on the carpet. It meant by the time we arrived at the studio for our rehearsal, Ashleigh and I were relaxed and free to concentrate on our act.

'Wow!' I said to myself, when I laid eyes on the set. 'If only the others could see this.'

I looked up as a suspended platform with a revolving chair on it was lowered to the floor. All around, a host of spotlights cut through the gloom, while a projection of an inferno filled the backdrop. Ashleigh and I would be making a seriously dramatic entrance, but it was only as we tried the descent for ourselves that I realised the pets would of course be watching on the big night. It felt good to know that Obi, Indi, my mum and the others would be witnessing this live. They couldn't be in the seats with the audience – with the exception of me the place had a no-pet policy – but I knew they'd be glued to the screen at home and rooting for us every step of the way.

The rehearsal itself went without a hitch. That's if we didn't include the problem with the judges' table. There was nothing wrong with it, as such, but it reminded me of that very first time I attempted a raised crossing in agility. The flashbacks were intense and threatened to destroy my confidence. I had visions of putting a paw wrong and crashing into the judges. As a result, I simply couldn't get across without pulling up. I was determined to do it, of course ... but then our time on stage ran out.

'You'll be fine when it really matters,' Ashleigh said to reassure me. 'I have every faith in you.'

That night, I dreamed that the show's producers had decided to make a last-minute change to the format of the final. Tomorrow, we discovered, we would be competing in *Britain's Got Talent – on Ice!*

I was fitted with two pairs of skates and shoved in front of the audience, the judges and the cameras. Naturally, it was a disaster. While Ashleigh turned and pirouetted effortlessly, I glided helplessly past her and fell off the far side of the stage.

In one sense, it was a relief to wake up the next morning. In another, I did so with my heart in my mouth when I realised what we'd be facing in the evening.

'I think we both need some fresh air,' said Ashleigh after breakfast. 'Do you fancy a walk, Pudsey?'

I'll never know why people sometimes present this to their dogs as a question. It's the same as saying 'Would you like a free holiday in the Caribbean?' There can only be one answer, which is why I responded by racing to grab my black sparkly leash.

It was nice to explore a new environment. The hotel was just off the high street with a park on the other side. There was nothing remarkable about any of it. Even so, that walk will stay with me for ever.

'Hey, look! Isn't that Pudsey off of *X Factor*?'

'No, stupid. He's from *It's Me or the Dog.*'

'You're both wrong! He's on *Britain's Got Talent*!'

Ashleigh and I had only just crossed the high street when the first people to recognise us asked for our autographs. Well, not mine, exactly, but Ashleigh was happy to oblige. The same thing happened again at the gates to the park, and several times around the little pond. I lost count of the number of individuals who patted and admired me, or asked to take a photograph. It also meant I was too busy to chase the ducks.

'You don't want to do that anyway,' one of the mallards warned me as I strained against the leash. The duck drew my attention to a man with a camera who was lurking nearby. By now, I had begun to recognise the paparazzi. 'Can you imagine tomorrow's headlines if you took us out? "FOWL PLAY ... Feathers Fly as Dancing Dog Goes Quackers".'

The duck seemed a little too pleased with the imaginary headline, but it was a fair point and I backed off accordingly. But one last thing bothered me.

'How did you know who I am?' I asked, as Ashleigh led me away.

'Oh, we read the papers,' the duck called after me. 'They're always blowing through here.'

We spent the rest of the day in the hotel. Penny was keen to make sure that Ashleigh and I stayed calm and relaxed. Which of course proved to be impossible. Eventually, after Penny and Grandma decided they'd had enough of watching us both pace the room, we set off for the studio.

'Once we're there,' said Penny, 'you won't have time to worry.'

I didn't usually doubt her word. This time, I saw no end to the tension I was feeling. As soon as we arrived, it became clear that we were set to take part in a huge event. The press were everywhere. I even noticed a news helicopter buzzing overhead. Within moments of arriving, we were ushered through the crowds waiting for the studio doors to open, and escorted straight to our dressing room. My plan was to settle in the corner and get some kip, but the press officer had other ideas. As soon as Ashleigh had finished in hair and make-up and climbed into her catsuit, we were taken to a conference room upstairs where a string of journalists and television crews were waiting. I had to admire Ashleigh for the effort she made to speak to them all in turn. It went on for so long I'm surprised she didn't lose her voice. I just rested in her arms, trying as my mum had suggested to imagine a special place to which I could transport myself and escape the tension. But still nothing came to mind. I even tried to snooze with my eyes open. It was only when the final interview wrapped that I accepted such a feat was frankly impossible.

I also realised that this was no time to be a stupid dog. I would have plenty of opportunity for that, but now I needed to show that I was one of a kind.

'Pudsey and Ashleigh?' asked one of the production crew, who had just hurried in to find us. She was wearing a headset. Judging by her pained expression, the poor woman was clearly being yelled at over the airwaves by someone in the director's gallery.

'It's Ashleigh and Pudsey,' said Penny, who had been in the background throughout the course of the interviews. On this occasion, however, there was no time for corrections.

'I hope both of you are ready, because you're live in two minutes!'

24

Executing the extremely complicated pasa-quadruplée.
It might look like I'm just running through Ashleigh's
arms, but trust me, if I put a paw wrong here
I'm a dog's dinner.

W hen the stage lights go on, it's easy to think that nobody is watching. The glare from the lamps at the front is so intense that you can't see anything beyond. It meant when Ashleigh and I descended from the rafters, we could've been all on our own.

As we threw ourselves into our performance to the deafening and dramatic strains of the *Mission Impossible* theme, I didn't think about the studio audience or the millions of viewers at home. I had in my mind just a handful of friends who I knew would be glued to the screen. I could just imagine Obi, Indi and my mum in a crescent around the television, along with Brad and his reprobate pals. It fired me up to think about them rooting for us, and kept me going all the way to what I hoped would be our show-stopping moment.

'You can do it,' Ashleigh urged me under her breath as we sprang from the stage and circled towards the judges' panel. I knew what had to be done. With Ashleigh guiding me, and to gasps of surprise, I scrambled up the steep side ramp. 'Be lucky, Pudsey!'

All four judges were facing me, with expressions on their faces that ranged from joy, laughter and astonishment to apparent indifference. Despite Simon's expression, I detected a look of warmth in his eyes when I made it onto the level surface. As I did so, however, my silver dog tag caught on the lip of the ramp. I was moving at such a lick that it didn't stop me, but I heard something ping away from my collar as it stretched. I glanced down, and saw Brad's lucky charm drop away. There was no time to stop, or consider what this meant. I just figured that without that extra life I might well have slipped into disaster. Instead, I reached the ramp on the other side and tore back onto the stage for the finale of our performance.

We finished with a gymnastic tumble that could have been car-crash television. It involved a great deal of balance, especially in the face of such applause, but together we pulled it off. My heart was hammering and if I could sweat it would've been pouring from my brow. Instead, I adopted the cutest face I could muster and relished the response from the audience and the judges.

'We did it,' I whispered under the roar of applause. 'We made it to the end!'

Once again I looked directly into Simon's eyes. He was smiling and clapping, then paused to spread open the neck of his shirt. I figured this meant we must've raised the temperature in the studio, and hoped we'd done likewise with the people back home. Because this time, once the judges had passed comment, the phone lines were open for a public vote.

Our fate, I realised when we finally left the stage, was now in the hands of the nation.

We had put on the performance of a lifetime. That's what Penny told us in the wings. Grandma nodded in agreement, her eyes never leaving David Walliams. Ashleigh, meanwhile, had not stopped hugging me.

'I'm so proud of you, Pudsey,' she whispered. 'We've done everything we can.'

Watching the act that followed, the last to step out in front of the judges, I questioned whether everything was enough.

Jonathan and Charlotte were hugely talented singers. They'd put in a powerful performance every time, but this one was note perfect and brimming with raw passion. Ashleigh, Grandma and Penny watched with tears in their eyes. I was welling up on the inside. Still, I kept it together sufficiently to do my duty as a dog at times of high emotion and licked Ashleigh's face until she giggled and regained her composure. She joined in the applause, clearly pleased that they'd impressed both the judges and the audience. One glance in Penny's direction, however, told me she was convinced that we had just witnessed the winning act. I looked back at Ashleigh. She smiled bravely at me.

'Pudsey, I think we need a break,' she said. 'This is getting intense.'

We had half an hour before the results were announced. While the other acts milled about expectantly in the wings, Ashleigh slipped away and I followed close behind. The studio was a maze of corridors, many of which were out of bounds. Still, that didn't stop her from pushing through doors that probably should've been locked. It almost felt like a scene from Mission Impossible as we crept under meeting-room windows where studio

executives were locked in conversation. At one point, I wondered whether Ashleigh would climb through a roof hatch
and make her way along the ventilation shafts. To my
relief, she chose to head up the stairs instead, following
signs that I couldn't read. Eventually, we reached a fire exit.
I'm not sure what I was expecting when Ashleigh opened
the door. A balcony, perhaps, or access to the upper level of
a car park.

Instead, we stepped out onto a magnificent roof garden
overlooking London under the stars.

'This will do just nicely,' she said, and pushed through
a mass of ferns towards a clearing marked out by grasses
and bamboo. 'There's nobody here but us.'

I looked up and around in awe. A mothball moon hung
over the capital. Pigeons could be heard cooing from lofts
around the television studio, and a police siren howled
in the streets below. At that moment, knowing that people
everywhere were voting for their favourite act, it felt as if
Ashleigh and I had found a little patch of paradise. There
was a bench in the clearing. It looked out over Wembley
Stadium's arch, lit up against the night sky, and across to
the heart of the city beyond. Together, we sat and admired
the view.

'I never dreamed we'd get this far,' said Ashleigh.
'Whatever happens now, I'm so happy that we had this
opportunity.'

'Me too,' I thought to myself, and wondered whether
she had any more ham sandwich squares in her utility belt.

We remained there in silence for a while. It was a clear
night with banks of stars overhead and a crisp chill in the

air. Ashleigh wrapped her arm around me and I cuddled up close to her. Our moment of peace only came to an end when voices could be heard from the doorway behind us. I turned to see a flashlight cut through the gloom, and then point in our direction.

'There you are!' Penny appeared in the company of a security guard, looking mightily relieved to see us. 'We were worried about you!'

Ashleigh rose to her feet. I hopped off the bench and stood beside her.

'There's no need to fret,' she chuckled. 'Not when I have Pudsey.'

Our pause for breath on that roof garden was just what was needed. Not only did we have a chance to take time out from the drama of the show, I left feeling closer to Ashleigh than ever before. We had been through a great deal to get this far. Whatever happened next, we would leave with a bond that many dogs and their owners could only dream of achieving.

I also had a chance to mark my territory against a palm tree as we headed back inside. After that, I was ready for us to take our places for the results.

Back on stage, I jumped into Ashleigh's arms. She stood with her head bowed expectantly, as did all the other finalists who stepped out around her. One by one, Pant and Beg addressed each act and revealed whether or not they had made it to the top three. Every time, they preceded the news with a pause that felt as if time itself had stopped. If an act hadn't gained enough votes, the spotlight illuminating them went out.

By the time the Geordie duo came to us, the stage was looking pretty dark.

'Ashleigh and Pudsey,' said the shorter one. 'You ... ' This time the pause went on for so long I was tempted to bark to bring them back to the matter at hand. I could just imagine the pets back home hurling things at the screen and urging them to get on with it. 'You are in the top three!'

I heard the result but struggled to take it in. This was on account of being smothered with love and pride by Ashleigh.

'Unbelievable!' she whispered, composing herself as the last acts learned their fate.

A minute later, all we could do was stand and hope as Pant and Beg dispatched the phenomenal choir, Only Boys Aloud, which left just us against Charlotte and Jonathan.

'Good luck,' whispered Ashleigh to the pair as we were gathered together for the final announcement. I didn't think they needed to call upon luck. As an act, Charlotte and Jonathan had huge support. We could hear people in the audience calling out encouragement to them. I did hear several voices calling out my name, but forced myself to keep an open mind. This way, I decided, I couldn't be disappointed.

'So, this is it,' said Beg, or Pant. 'After thousands of auditions, five semi-finals and one incredible final, it comes down to just two acts. And one of you is about to walk away with half a million pounds, as well as a place at the Royal Variety Performance, in front of Her Majesty the Queen.'

The money, of course, meant nothing to me. Dogs don't have bank accounts, after all. It was the possibility that I might get to sniff bottoms with the royal corgis that set my heart racing.

'The winner of *Britain's Got Talent* 2012 is ...'

This time, I thought I was ready for the almighty pause that came beforehand. It was probably a mistake to hold my breath, but I got through it by reflecting on all the trials and obstacles we had faced to get to where we stood just then, in front of the nation. In a way, life for Ashleigh and me had been one big agility course, and here we were at the finishing line. It had been a unique, incredible time, and now we were set to learn what lay ahead.

'Ashleigh and Pudsey!'

The studio spun before my eyes. We had won! Not only that, I had deprived my lungs of oxygen for a second too long. I took a massive breath, only to have it squeezed right out of me as Ashleigh broke down with tears of joy.

'We did it!' she sobbed. 'And it's all down to you, Puds!'

25

Pant (or is it Beg?) congratulates us on our victory. I've just spotted a spare chunk of ham sandwich.

B ackstage, it was bedlam.

It felt as if a thousand and one people wanted to come up to congratulate us. Every act was very gracious in defeat, and Ashleigh hugged them all. When I saw Penny and Grandma through the hordes, I hopped down to see them. Penny was thrilled and overwhelmed, and Grandma was clearly chuffed, although her more urgent mission was to get an autograph from David Walliams.

'Congratulations, Pudsey,' said the man himself, when Grandma finally cornered him.

'It isn't too late for babies,' she said, which drew his attention away from me somewhat. When David's eyebrows shot up in response, it was hard to tell whether he was appalled or intrigued. Fortunately, Penny was on hand to shelter him. It left me to slip away and seek out Ashleigh once more.

By now, however, there were so many people clamouring for her attention that I couldn't get anywhere close. What's more, being so low to the ground it was a struggle not to be squashed. Eventually, I gave up and sat quietly on the sidelines. It was from there that I caught the eye of Amanda Holden and Alesha Dixon, who were talking to one of the show's producers. They broke off when they saw me and made their way through the throng.

'You have such a shining future ahead of you,' said Amanda, crouching to pet me. All I could think was that Obi would've forfeited every dog treat for a year for the chance to be this close to her.

'You're adorable,' added Alesha, and leaned forward to kiss me on the forehead.

I'm sure you understand that this made me incredibly happy. I wanted to find out if either of them had any female dogs at home who would like some time in my company. Unfortunately, before I could figure out a way to ask, someone very important-looking ushered them both away.

When I finally caught up with Ashleigh, I jumped into her arms immediately. I never wanted to be apart from her again. We were going through the same emotions together, after all. We had just won the biggest variety show in the country, and the feeling was intense. Just as I was settling into her arms, Penny hurried across to speak to Ashleigh.

'You'll never believe this, but Simon Cowell has asked you both to drop by his dressing room. Normally he leaves the studio straight away, but I've just received a note from him.' Penny showed Ashleigh the handwritten card. 'The man himself is waiting to have his picture taken with you and Pudsey!'

'You're kidding?' Ashleigh looked stunned, but not for long because one of the production team cut through the crowds just then, looking very relieved to have found us.

'The ITV2 after-show is waiting to talk to you,' she said breathlessly. 'You're needed in Studio B right away!'

That evening, as we completed one television interview and went straight into another, I realised how much our lives were set to change. For one thing, Ashleigh had just won half a million pounds. I tried to calculate how many rawhide chews that would buy us, but lost count when I reached double figures.

As well as the prize money, we also earned an awful lot of attention straight away from showbiz agents and managers. They approached us in between interviews, stopping us in corridors to pitch why we should pick them to represent us. Fortunately, Penny was around to handle them all. Like Ashleigh, she saw a bright future for us. She just wanted to be sure that we were backed by people who respected us and weren't just out to make a quick buck.

'I can't believe this is happening,' whispered Ashleigh, as we were directed into yet another room. This time, to our surprise and delight, we were greeted by cheers from every act who had appeared in the finals, as well as the entire production crew.

As parties go, I think even Obi, Indi and Handsome Brad would've been hard-pressed to rival this one. Absolutely everyone hand-fed me buffet food, while Ashleigh hit the makeshift dance floor to celebrate our win. Even Grandma got into the groove, which was wonderful to see. I loved every moment. People chatted and laughed and toasted each other's good fortune. Despite being exhausted by the events of the day, we were among the last to leave.

In the studio lobby, however, the receptionist called us over and relayed a message that had been left at the desk.

'Mr Cowell is still in his dressing room,' she said. 'He's been waiting to see you for hours.'

A collective gasp went up from Ashleigh, Penny and Grandma.

'I completely forgot!' cried Ashleigh.

'Are we in trouble?' asked Grandma.

Penny looked back at the receptionist, but she had just taken a call on her headset.

Nervously, we made our way back through the building. It had emptied out considerably, but several cleaning staff were able to point us in the right direction. Finally, we reached Simon's dressing-room door. Ashleigh raised her hand to knock, only to pause and turn to Penny.

'I can't do it,' she whispered. 'I feel awful that we're so late.'

'Then don't make him wait any longer,' hissed Penny, and knocked for her.

I can only think that Simon punctuated his whole life with extended pauses, because yet again an age passed before he answered.

'Enter!' we heard him say eventually, that single word making him sound thoroughly fed up.

Taking a breath, with me in her arms once more, Ashleigh clicked open the door.

'Mr Cowell, I'm so sorry! We got caught up with interviews. Then there was a party and we just forgot ourselves.'

'So I see.'

Simon was sitting on one side of a leather armchair, resting his head against one hand. I glanced around. It wasn't exactly a dressing room, I thought to myself, given that it was about the size of a Bond villain's secret volcano hideaway.

'It's my fault,' Penny offered. 'This whole experience has just been so overwhelming.'

Simon didn't answer. Instead, his eyes turned to me.

'I hope you had a good time celebrating your win.'

Nobody spoke for a moment. We just hung our heads.

'I don't know what else I can say,' whispered Ashleigh, her voice wavering.

'Then don't!' declared Simon, which prompted us all to look up. He gestured at the space on the sofa. 'Just bring me this amazing dog. I can't wait to meet Pudsey properly!'

At once, the tension in the room turned to relief. Simon flashed a smile at me as Ashleigh set me down. I jumped right up next to the man himself and barked once in sheer happiness. Simon handed Penny his phone, and together with Ashleigh we posed for a picture.

'Nobody's going to believe this really happened,' said Ashleigh, grinning alongside me.

'Oh they will,' said Simon, as he reclaimed the phone and prepared to tweet the picture. 'And everyone's going to see a lot more of you two in future. As soon as I saw you both, I just knew there was something magical in what you had to offer. Now you've arrived on the national stage, I have every belief that you and Pudsey can conquer the world!'

'Do you really think so?' asked Ashleigh, clearly stunned.

'Sure,' Simon said. 'Pudsey's a natural. I see a career in television, musicals, the movies … even a book.' He leaned forward, checked he had our full attention and then held his hands apart. 'Guys, what do you say to Pudsey's own autobiDOGraphy?'

I glanced at Penny. It was clear that Simon had given this a great deal of thought, which is why it was brave of her to spell out the obvious.

'It's a lovely idea,' she said hesitantly, 'but Pudsey can't write.'

'He's a dog,' Grandma chipped in. 'They're illiterate.'

Simon swatted away this minor hiccup.

'If the dog can learn to dance, he can learn to put pen to paper. Leave it with me. We have people. Nothing is impossible in my world. It's all about making dreams come true.'

'Well, you've certainly done that for us this evening,' said Ashleigh, facing me. 'And we'll never forget it for the rest of our lives!'

26

Grandma, ~~David Walliams'~~ our biggest fan,
with Ashleigh. I took this photo, as it happens –
I'm a regular Bonio Testino.

Back at the budget hotel, we were all too excited to turn in. Even Grandma showed no signs of flagging. For ages she stayed up with Ashleigh and Penny to relive the evening's events. She had a signed photograph of David Walliams in her hand, addressing it from time to time as if he was actually in the room with us. It was only when she found the mini-bar that Penny suggested we all really needed to get a grip.

'Ashleigh and Pudsey are booked to be on the breakfast television sofa at the crack of dawn,' she told her. 'It won't look good if you stumble out of the taxi with a hangover. The photographers will have a field day!'

'She's right,' chuckled Ashleigh.

Grandma eyed the clutch of miniature bottles she had hauled out of the fridge. Then, with a sigh, she returned all but one.

'Maybe a nightcap, then. Just to help me settle.'

Even with the lights off, I struggled to get any shuteye. Lying on blankets beside Ashleigh's bed, I listened to her breathing grow heavier, and was pleased when she finally found sleep. The day had been as long and exhausting as it was life-changing. It had opened up a whole world of opportunities, and offered me a chance to dance for a long time to come.

Unlike Ashleigh, however, one thing had happened to

me that evening I feared I would regret. I'd managed to block it from my mind in the excitement of winning, but now, lying in the darkness and the silence, I couldn't ignore the fact that our victory had cost me something very precious and irreplaceable. Something that by rights belonged to Handsome Brad. He had loaned me the lucky charm to boost my confidence, only I had managed to use up the life it represented by crossing the judges' table in one piece.

'I'm toast,' I sighed to myself. 'That cat is going to kill me.'

Believe me, in my world you really don't want to displease the boss dog. It didn't matter that Brad happened to be a ginger tom. Back home, we lived by his rules, and if we broke them, we suffered the consequences.

For ages, I lay there wondering what I could do to make up for losing one of the cat's remaining nine lives. Would Brad settle for an autograph from Simon Cowell, or was I destined to serve as his bed warmer for the rest of my life? I even wondered whether he might do me physical harm for throwing away something so invaluable to him. Cats had a reputation for being brutal, which did little for my peace of mind.

It meant that when Ashleigh's alarm sounded, blaring out the *Flintstones* theme tune – because yet again she'd forgotten to change it – I had barely slept a wink.

Going on breakfast television is an honour, but I have to say the name was a bit misleading. Why? Because there wasn't any breakfast. Nothing. We were whisked onto the sofa, interviewed about how we felt the morning after our win, and then ushered out to a car that Simon had laid on for us. Now, I don't want to sound like a dog diva, it isn't in my breeding, but that wasn't breakfast television. It was just, well … television.

What's more, it didn't end there. I had thought we would be heading home straight after our appearance. Instead, Penny took a call from the show's press office and within minutes we were on our way to another interview.

'This is unbelievable,' said Ashleigh on the way. 'I can't take in how many people are interested in us!'

In a way, I wasn't sorry to be delayed in going back. It meant I didn't have to think about the moment when I'd face Handsome Brad. Just how did you break the news that you had lost a cat one of his lives? It wasn't like misplacing the remote control for the TV. That could be replaced. This was unique. It could only mean trouble for me.

We ended up spending the whole morning shuttling from one interview to the next, for television, radio, newspapers and websites. It wasn't just the British press who were desperate to speak to us, either. We faced journalists from all around the world. Ashleigh remained calm and collected, despite clearly swelling with pride, while I sat on her lap, smiled for the cameras, and wondered whether I should even bother going back to the house.

'Is everything OK, Pudsey?' asked Ashleigh eventually. 'You look as if you could curl up for a snooze.'

Frankly, I wanted to curl up and die, but that wasn't

going to happen. Instead, with our bags in the boot of the taxi, we finally left London and headed for home. The return journey was strange. We were going back to a familiar world, and yet things felt different. We were no longer simply a girl and her dog hoping to live a dream. We *were* living it now, and everyone knew our names. We discovered this for ourselves when we stopped at a motorway service station. It wasn't just Ashleigh who found herself crowded by people asking for her autograph. As soon as she let me onto a grass bank to stretch my legs, I was approached by a yapping terrier.

'Hey, it's the dog from the telly! You nailed it for the canine brotherhood last night, my friend. It's Pansy, right?'

'Pudsey,' I said to correct him.

'Yeah, whatever.' The terrier moved in to sniff my rear end. 'May I?'

'Be my guest.' I stood politely, despite showing a lack of interest in doing the same thing. Instead, I kept half an eye on Ashleigh as a clutch of children hurried over to see what all the fuss was about.

'Ah the sweet smell of success!' said the dog. 'So, how does it feel to be famous?'

I turned to face the terrier.

'Honestly?' I said. 'No different.'

'Really?' Clearly the dog didn't believe me. 'But you can't have a worry in the world!'

I pictured Handsome Brad, waiting for our return. Just then I didn't think anything that I could offer him would make up for the loss of one of his feline lives. It left me with no choice, I realised. There was nothing I could serve up to soften the news. All I could do was be truthful with him about what had happened, and offer an apology that came from the heart.

'I have to leave now,' I told the terrier, on seeing Ashleigh finish signing bits of paper, as well as people's hands and arms. 'I need to see a cat about something.'

'Be sure to kick his butt!' the terrier called after me, though I feared it would be the other way round.

27

Paws for Thought

In recent months I've travelled widely by plane. Here are my top three tips for dogs on the long-haul:

1. I realise this breaks dog rules, but resist the urge to pull a stupid face with your tongue hanging out when you have the photo taken for your pet passport. It makes life easier at customs.

2. Always turn left when you enter the aeroplane. Apparently the seats on the other side are for cattle.

3. Ignore what people say about jetlag. It's really no big deal. When did a dog ever have difficulty getting to sleep?

Outside the house, as the taxi driver unloaded the boot, I swore I heard the hum of a vacuum cleaner.

It seemed to be coming from the front room, but stopped as soon as Penny opened the yard gate. Maybe it was my sharp hearing, because nobody else appeared to notice. Instead, they opened the back door to be greeted enthusiastically by Indi and Obi.

'You did it!' Mum said, rushing out behind them to circle me wildly. 'We watched the whole thing, Pudsey. You both deserved to win!'

'Thanks,' I said, looking around nervously. 'Where's Brad?'

'Nursing a massive headache, I should think,' she told me. 'His friends are such a bad influence. Between them, they managed to bring round a canister of catnip spray. You know? The plant extract that kitties go crazy for. During the final, they played some stupid game where they squirted it every time Simon said he always wanted a dog like you.'

'I see,' I said. 'Was that a lot?'

My mum didn't reply directly, but she told me it could be quite a while before we saw the cat again. I was about to confess to her about my loss, but just then the collies bundled between us.

'Here he is!' cried Obi. 'The dog that melted the heart of a nation!'

'Let's not go overboard,' I said, smiling all the same. 'It's only me. Pudsey.'

Obi stopped in front of me and shook his head. It was a movement that went all the way down to the tip of his tail, because once a dog shakes we just can't stop.

'Now's not the time to be modest,' he said solemnly. 'You're set to be a superstar, man! It's time to live the dream. This house could do with a makeover for a start.'

'You need to pimp up the place,' Indi suggested, sharing Obi's excitement. 'I'm thinking chicken-flavoured wallpaper ... sofas of our own that we can sit on. And a massive fridge with paw-activated double doors.'

'We are going to party, baby!' said Obi, his tail wagging manically. 'In fact, we haven't really stopped since last night.'

I glanced at the open door.

'What's it like in there?' I asked. 'Penny won't be pleased if you've made a mess.'

'Well, it was in a bit of a state,' Indi confessed, 'but we have Smidgit to thank for the emergency clean-up operation. It's amazing how quickly and effectively thirty guinea pigs can tidy up a house. Even the cats who'd gatecrashed the party recognised it was a no-brainer, which is why they agreed not to go on the rampage when Obi let them out.'

It was a lot to take in, but no more than we had been faced with since leaving for the final. Padding inside the house, it seemed that the pets had indeed done a great job in making everything look as good as new. Penny didn't bat an eyelid, although she did stop in the front room and sniff the air suspiciously.

'Is it just me,' she asked, and crossed the room to fluff a cushion, 'but does it smell odd in here?'

Both collies looked to the floor.

'It's just you,' said Obi.

'There was no party,' added Indi, clearly unable to keep a secret to herself. 'We didn't touch the catnip! That's not our thing. Nor did we scoff the crisps from the cupboard ... OK! Maybe the crisps!'

'Calm down, everyone,' I told them. 'Even if you wanted to make a confession, Penny can't understand you.'

'What's with the whining?' Ashleigh asked them, having seen Grandma into the spare room where she'd been planning on pinning up her photograph of David. 'Did you miss us?'

She petted both collies, and also my mum, before facing Penny directly. For a moment, the pair just stared at one another in silence. Everything felt so normal, here in our own home, and yet so much had changed. Then Ashleigh and Penny pressed their palms to their faces and let out a shriek of delight that startled us all.

'It still feels so unreal!' cried Ashleigh, jumping up and down. At the same time, the home phone started ringing.

'Not again,' my mum complained. 'We've had message after message from friends and family, not to mention all the bouquets outside the front door. Everyone wants to congratulate the pair of you.'

I sighed to myself and looked to the window.

'I'm trying to relish the moment,' I told her. 'But there's something on my mind that's stopping me.'

'What's that?' she asked.

I was aware that both collies were also waiting for me to answer. I didn't know what they'd make of the fact that I had taken a life from the cat and lost it. It wasn't a very dog-like thing to do, after all. Still, I thought they needed to know why I had returned home with the weight of the world on my shoulders, so I told them all about the charm. But instead of pouring scorn on me, both Obi and Indi shrugged as if these things happened all the time.

'It's just a life,' said Obi, a little unhelpfully. 'As he's lucky enough to have nine, I'm sure he can live without one.'

'Brad's used up quite a few already,' I told him. 'You don't get to be boss dog without taking some knocks along the way.'

'I see,' said Indi, and her face promptly lit up with a suggestion. 'I know,' she said. 'We can make him one!'

'A life?' I asked. 'From what?'

'Oh, I don't know.' Indi seemed frustrated by such details. 'How about some silver foil and a safety pin?'

I considered the idea for a moment. Kind as it was that the dogs had my best interests at heart, there really was just one option available to me.

'I'm going to find Handsome Brad,' I told them. 'I need to speak to him, dog to cat.'

Whenever Brad paid us a visit, which was pretty much every day, he always appeared on the fence dividing our garden from Shredder's turf. I don't know how he did it. Either he'd lost some lives there as well, or simply got the bulldog's measure. Nevertheless, I reckoned I should set off to look for him in that direction.

I gave the guinea pigs' run a wide berth. As much as I wanted to see Smidgit, it was important to me that I should take responsibility for losing one of Brad's lives first. Now, most dogs would find it hard to scramble up onto a fence and balance there. Fortunately, I'd had a great deal of practice. It meant I was free to reason with the bulldog, who had noticed my sudden appearance and was busy flinging spittle everywhere.

'Shredder, can I ask for your understanding here,' I said.

'You won't get nothing like that from me!' he raged, jumping repeatedly against the fence. 'I saw you on TV at the weekend. Prancing about on the stage. You're an embarrassment, mate. Dogs like you should be ashamed of yourself!'

'Yes, well, thanks for that, Shredder. But the thing is I borrowed something for the show. A good luck charm belonging to Handsome Brad.'

Shredder stopped leaping at me for a moment.

'One of his nine lives?' he asked. 'Them things are like gold dust to a cat.'

'Well, the thing is, I've lost it.'

I had never seen Shredder with all the rage knocked out of him, but I did just then. The bulldog simply looked up at me in stunned silence.

'Dude,' he said eventually. 'You're in trouble.'

'I know, I know,' I said, well aware of the rules. 'Never cross a cat because they'll always strike back with great vengeance and furious anger.'

'They certainly know how to bear a grudge,' he agreed. 'So, what are you going to do?'

I told Shredder I wanted to speak to Brad, and just be open and honest with him.

'Are you crazy?' Shredder paced back and forth. 'If it was me I'd have all the windows locked down and never leave the house again. Cats can be totally cold-blooded when it comes to revenge. You'll be dicing with death, my friend.'

'It's the right thing to do,' I told him.

'If you've got the guts,' he said. 'You know, sometimes the wrong thing's a whole lot easier to do. You might want to consider just lying low for the rest of your life.'

'I can't do that.' I looked down at Shredder, feeling as if I had the high ground here in more ways than one. 'But if I'm going to find Brad I need to pass through your garden safely. So, I'm asking you, as one dog to another, to give me this chance.'

Shredder looked down for a moment, and then back up at me.

'I don't know, Pudsey,' he said. 'I want to say yes, but it's my territorial instincts, see. I'm not sure I can hold them back. If you jump down here and the red mist appears in front of my eyes, I can't be responsible for my actions.'

I held his gaze, seeking some kind of understanding.

'Please, Shredder. Let me through and we'll never speak of it again.'

'So you won't tell no one else?' asked the bulldog, having first checked we couldn't be overheard. 'I've got a name for myself around here as a formidable hard nut.'

'I've no intention of ruining your reputation,' I said, and prepared to give it a shot. 'Now be a good doggie,' I added, as Shredder watched me cautiously. 'Let Pudsey pass.'

I dropped down soundlessly, and adopted the crouch position in case I had to make a hasty retreat. Shredder snarled involuntarily. It was clear that the hellhound inside him was straining to pounce, but somehow he held his ground. Keeping eye contact with him at all times, I sidestepped wide around the bulldog.

'Brad lives in the house across the road from here,' growled Shredder. 'Also three doors to the right, and the one five to the left on this side. Depending on what each house has to offer.'

'Right,' I said, still increasing the distance between us. 'And thanks.'

Shredder responded by narrowing his eyes.

'I'm struggling here, pal. You need to hurry. Go!'

I noted how his entire body began to quiver with his warning, and turned tail just as a sense of fury at my presence overwhelmed him. Fortunately, I had a big enough advantage to reach the yard gate and clamber over it before the furious beast could reach me. It was like leaving behind a different dog, but I was grateful to Shredder for the break.

Padding out onto the road, I looked one way and then the other, wondering where to begin. I didn't have to think long, however, because just then a voice called out my name. It was one that caused a shudder to pass right through me.

'Well, look who's back,' Handsome Brad called out. 'If it isn't Twinkle Toes!'

I looked around, finally spotting him at the front door two doors down. It wasn't one that Shredder had suggested. Looking at the milk bottle on the step that Brad had clawed open, I guessed the house just happened to have something to provide him with at that moment.

'Hey,' I said, smiling through my nerves. 'I've been looking for you.'

'Well, here I am.' The ginger tom paused to lap the cream from the neck of the bottle. 'Oh, that tastes good. Nothing like a drop of milk to cure a thick head.'

'I heard you had quite a party,' I said, and dared to pad a little closer.

'A two-day bender, my friend. Would've been rude not to celebrate your victory in style.' He stopped to take another drink. 'I see my charm helped you overcome your nerves,' he said, wiping milk from his whiskers with one paw.

'It saw me through to the end,' I said, and hesitated for a second. 'Brad, there's something I need to tell you. That moment when I crossed the judges' panel.'

'You made it safe and sound,' Brad cut in. 'A sweet move.'

I looked away, and then willed myself to meet his eyes.

'I think I may have used your life to get across without an accident.'

It might well have been that every bird in the trees fell silent at that moment. I certainly didn't hear a single chirp or trill. If anything, I picked up on the sound of Brad swallowing with difficulty.

'What?' he asked, without blinking.

I repeated what I had said, followed by a profound apology.

'Believe me, Brad. Had I known, I would've left it behind in the dressing room and taken my chances.'

Brad breathed out long and hard.

'You do know what this means, don't you?' He prowled towards me, stopping so his head was alongside mine. Then he turned to face me side on. 'For every life lost,' he whispered, in a way that sounded like a major threat, 'there's a price to pay.'

28

'Dogs never bite me. Just humans.'
Marilyn Monroe

I didn't know what to say. Standing there with Handsome Brad circling me, I just reminded myself that being truthful was the only thing I could've done.

'How many lives do you have left?' I asked nervously.

'After what happened at the party?' he said. 'Probably just the one.'

Brad's breath smelled of stale catnip and fresh milk. I wanted to step away, but felt powerless to do so. Although I was bigger than Brad, I lacked his killer instinct. If I provoked him, I knew he would go further than any dog would ever dare, and might cause me serious harm. All I could do was let him toy with me, while I simply spoke to him from the heart.

'I know how much that charm meant to you,' I said. 'I'd rather have tumbled into the judges than be facing you like this now.'

Brad stopped circling, right in front of me, and turned to face me directly. His eyes narrowed, causing my blood to chill. Then, to my surprise, he began to chuckle to himself.

'I dare say you would've made it across perfectly well without it,' he told me, seemingly unable to get a grip on his amusement. 'We watched the whole thing on TV, Pudsey. The charm didn't make the slightest difference to your performance. It was sheer bad luck that your dog tag got caught at the top of the ramp. If anything, you recovered with a great deal of poise! I like to think I showed you how to do that.'

I looked at Brad for a second, struggling to process what this meant.

'Are you suggesting that my inner cat saved the day?'

Slowly, the ginger tom regained his composure. Still smiling, he shrugged and continued to pace.

'The truth hurts, huh?'

I found myself staring at the tarmac, reflecting on what he'd just said.

'But you still lost a life,' I said. 'All because of me.'

Handsome Brad came around full circle. He seemed to size up for a moment what this meant to him, before shrugging as though it was something he could handle.

'One's enough for most creatures in this world. I guess I'll just have to make the most of it.'

With his tail raised and swishing like a snake charmer's cobra, the ginger tom returned to the milk bottle.

'So, what price do I have to pay?' I asked, just to clarify so I could sleep at night.

'Already settled,' said Brad, before extending a claw to puncture the foil top of the next bottle. 'Every cat around here knows about the dancing dog in my pack. A dog that landed half a million pounds in prize money on a national television talent show. It turns out they're seriously impressed, Pudsey. Especially when I tell them I taught you everything you know.' The cat turned to check that I'd understood him correctly.

'What about Ashleigh?' I asked, and cleared my throat.

'Oh, she helped,' Brad replied casually. 'But ultimately you couldn't have done it without me.'

I took a step back, as if that might help me get a grip on what was going on here.

'Can I ask one more thing?'

'Sure.'

'Why do you want everyone to think you're behind our victory?'

Brad seemed pleased that I had finally raised the matter.

'Right now,' he said, 'all across this neighbourhood, there are cats trying to teach the dogs in their pack how to stand on their hind legs. Listen carefully and you can hear them out in their gardens, putting the poor mutts through their paces with the high jumps and the twists and turns. It's hilarious, Pudsey! They're doomed to failure, of course. Which can only reflect very, very well on me.'

I nodded as he spoke, beginning to understand now.

'So, you'd no longer be boss dog just at our house ...' I suggested. 'Your respect would spread across all the streets and households around town?'

Handsome Brad looked satisfied with my summary.

'Ever heard of the Mafia?' he asked. 'Cats operate a very similar organisational structure. Nothing's official, but everyone knows who calls the shots.'

'Wow,' I said, having just learned something new. 'Dogs couldn't do that. We thrive on being told what to do.'

In response, Brad glanced up at the late afternoon sun, which was beginning to slip away, and suggested it was high time we headed back to my house to insulate a radiator.

It wasn't me who decided that we should avoid taking the short cut across Shredder's turf. With just one life left, Brad felt it was no longer worth taking such a risk.

'From now on I'll be taking things even easier than before,' he told me. 'As a cat who commands respect far and wide, it would be, uh, inappropriate not to wind down at my age.'

I looked across at him as we trotted along the pavement.

'What are you? Nine, ten years old?'

'I'm in my prime,' he told me. 'As a cat, that earns me the right to sleep throughout the day in the warmest spots.'

'I'm six,' I told him. 'Right now it feels like my whole life is ahead of me.'

'It certainly is,' Brad nodded in agreement. 'After what you've achieved, and with Simon Cowell behind you, you'll go further than any dog could ever imagine.'

I found myself laughing at this. It still felt completely unreal. And now, having come home, it almost seemed as if it had never happened at all.

It was only when we turned a corner that I realised things had in fact changed beyond belief. Instead of a sleepy road where squirrels scampered through the trees, we found neighbours and locals heading from both directions towards our front gate.

'What is this?' I asked, alarmed by so much activity. 'A zombie strike?'

'Zombies don't carry cards and gifts,' Brad pointed out. 'They don't tend to laugh and chatter either.'

Our front door was open, I realised, as people filed in. I heard music strike up from inside, and recognised the tune immediately.

'It's that man singing in the rain again,' I told Brad, and began to hum along. 'I've loved this song all my life.'

Brad jumped up onto a low wall to take a better look at what was going on.

'I'm not sure my head can handle another party,' he told me. 'Then again, how many times does a dog in my pack win *Britain's Got Talent*?'

I looked up at him.

'Ashleigh and Penny didn't mention a party,' I said. 'Although I suppose Grandma could be behind it. She's worse than you and your gang when it comes to raising the roof.'

'Whoever's responsible,' said Brad, 'there's one thing missing right now.'

'What's that?' I asked.

'You.'

29

Home.

I recognised lots of people in our hallway, kitchen and front room. The place was packed. Children squeezed between adults, chasing each other from room to room, while the buzz of chatter and laughter over the music was intense.

'Here he is,' said Obi when I found the collies. 'The dog du jour.'

'What is that?' asked Indi, turning to him. 'Spanish?'

'Duh,' said Obi, still grinning at me. 'Actually I think it's Dutch.'

'What's going on here?' I asked.

'What does it look like?' Indi invited me to look around. 'A surprise party, of course! You and Ashleigh might be set to become national treasures, but let's not forget you're local heroes too.'

My mum appeared just then. She looked at me, with Handsome Brad close behind, and sighed in relief.

'So, have you settled things?' she asked me, as the cat spotted a toddler clutching a sandwich.

'Will you excuse me for a moment?' asked Brad, as the toddler stumbled onwards, trailing the sandwich in his fist. 'Supper's just arrived.'

We watched the ginger tom stalk after the little boy, snatching mouthfuls from the sandwich whenever he wasn't watching.

'Brad and I are fine now,' I assured my mum. 'Our win's seen him earn promotion amongst all the cats in the neighbourhood.'

Mum nodded like she understood.

'Let me guess,' she said. 'Brad is claiming all the credit for your performance.'

'In a way, he laid down his life for me,' I told her. 'So long as Brad's happy with the outcome then so am I.'

As we spoke I caught sight of Ashleigh. She was laughing with her school friends in the corner. Having sacrificed so much time to train with me, it was great to see her catching up with her social life again. I knew that with Simon's support we would soon need to call upon a whole new set of dance routines, but for now it was time to unwind and celebrate with the people in our lives who mattered the most. It made me realise there was one individual I had yet to see. There had been so many who had helped Ashleigh and me to live our dream, but just one who was responsible for making it happen. Without Smidgit's drive and determination, Ashleigh would never have known how much I longed to become a dancer.

'Here he comes!' she cried, spotting me cross the garden. 'On my count, everyone, let's show Pudsey what we can do!'

I cleared the hedge to find Smidgit at the very centre of a line of guinea pigs. Each one was evenly spaced from the other, and they remained that way when they embarked upon one of the most complicated line dancing sequences I had ever seen them perform.

'Is this for me?' I asked, as Smidgit called out every step and turn.

'Join in!' she replied. 'It's a party, right?'

I glanced over my shoulder, well aware that people could see me from the windows. In a strange way, knowing I had an audience made me all the more enthusiastic about jumping in. That was how Smidgit had first made Grandma, Ashleigh and Penny realise what I really wanted to do. What's more, as I jumped into the sequence, it felt as if I had come full circle.

Sure enough, a few people noticed me out in the garden, seemingly shuffling about on my own. I wasn't embarrassed, however. Just happy and in good company.

'That was great!' I said when we finished, and jumped up on my hind legs to show my appreciation.

At once, all the guinea pigs cooed at me. Some even tried to mimic the move, without much success.

'Will you teach us how to do that one day?' asked Smidgit. 'None of us want to step in front of the television cameras like you, but we're always keen to push the limits of our craft.'

'Of course,' I said, admiring her outlook. 'We'll need a lot of ham sandwiches, of course.'

Smidgit tittered and scuttled to the front of the run. Her coat, always in good condition, just then looked absolutely stunning. It curled outwards at the ends, with what appeared to be frosting at the tips. I wondered whether the shed really did contain heaps of straw and sawdust, as you'd expect to find in a guinea pigs' sleeping quarters. Judging by Smidgit's immaculate appearance, it looked more like they ran a grooming parlour in there with driers and mirrors framed by light bulbs.

'We watched the highlights on television while cleaning up,' she told me. 'Congratulations, Pudsey. You and Ashleigh are shining stars!'

'Well, I don't know about that,' I said bashfully. 'But I couldn't have done it without you, Smidgit. I want to thank you and every single guinea pig for helping me. If there's anything I can do for you all, at any time, you just have to say the word.'

'Oh, stop it,' she said. 'We have food, shelter, space to run around and plenty of love and affection from Penny. We're simple creatures, Pudsey.'

'Ashleigh and I could always use some backing dancers,' I said hopefully, but Smidgit was insistent.

'Shouldn't you be getting back to the party?' she asked me, nodding towards the house. 'It sounds to me like Penny's about to make a speech.'

From the house, we could hear the sound of a champagne flute being tapped in a bid to get everyone's attention. It wasn't working terribly well, however. If anything, it was just making the collies kick off.

'Dogs will be dogs,' I said, turning back to Smidgit.

'Apart from dancing dogs. You can never predict what they'll do next.'

'Will you stop it?' I told her, laughing all the same. 'Wherever this thing takes us, this is always going to be home to me. That means no special treatment. I'm just Pudsey here, all right?'

'Understood.' Smidgit's eyes sparkled. She was clearly relishing this moment. Then her attention focused on something behind me. I turned to see Ashleigh making her way across the garden. Obi, Indi and my mum trotted close behind. Even Handsome Brad had dared to break cover to join them.

'There you are!' said Ashleigh, beaming at me. 'Everyone wants to meet you, Pudsey.'

'It seems you're the centre of attention,' said Brad under his breath. 'I'll let you have your moment.'

I glanced around at the pets. Everyone from the guinea pigs to the dogs were looking really pleased for me. I looked up at Ashleigh, who spread her hands wide. I didn't need any further invitation. I knew just what to do without even thinking about it, and jumped right into her arms.

'Pudsey,' she said, lifting her head high so I couldn't cover her face in dog lick, 'you mean so much to me, and I hope I mean the same to you, too!'

My response took the form of a hearty bark, which I repeated in case anybody hadn't heard me. This wasn't just because I loved Ashleigh with all my heart. I had also realised something really important as she turned to carry me into the house and the toast that awaited us. It had started with a word of advice that my mum offered, many years ago, and was one I'd never been able to put into practice.

Until now.

For I had found my special place at last. After so much searching, I didn't need to call upon my imagination for somewhere I could go when the going got tough. This was very real, and available to me at any time, right there in Ashleigh's arms.

Afterword

Success hasn't affected my life in the slightest.

'Pudsey,' people say to me. 'What's the secret behind your success?'

Of course, as you know by now, a dog can't get into a conversation and discuss the finer points of dedication, dreams and ambition. Even a dog that has defied all expectation and learned to dance for the nation. I can woof a lot and offer up a dreamy expression, but voicing my thoughts, recollections and opinions is just physically impossible.

Which is what persuaded me to write this book instead.

Without help and encouragement from Simon Cowell, none of this would've been possible. He really is a miracle maker, and I'm indebted to him for making it happen. Certainly I wouldn't be where I am today without his support and unswerving belief. Simon and I have become good friends, in fact. You may not have seen us spilling out of nightclubs, and that's because for all the glitz and glamour that surrounds us we share the same enjoyment of life's simple pleasures. We go on walks together, whenever my schedule allows. He throws me sticks. I chase them down and bring them back. Some say we have quite a bromance going. I prefer to think of myself as the man's best friend, but ultimately my heart belongs to Ashleigh.

Since winning *Britain's Got Talent*, we really have been living the dream. We've enjoyed flights on private jets, and made guest appearances on TV shows both here and across the pond (and we're not talking about the one in our local park). We've met all manner of stars, movers and shakers, all of whom marvel when we dance. Ashleigh and I continue to love every minute of it, and that's because we have each other when it all feels too good to be true. Even if it ended today, we'd always share memories of one amazing journey. For all the fame and fortune we've picked up on the way, however, I'm still plain old Pudsey back home. The only thing that's changed is the eight-foot-high security fence around the house to deter dognappers. Shredder was furious when that went up. As for what the future holds, I hope my achievements will encourage other pets to showcase their talents. A case in point is a ginger tom and his posse of old-school breakdancing moggies.* Believe me, it's a really impressive act. You might have witnessed Ashleigh and me take the world by storm, but the best is yet to come.

(*Did I say the right thing here, Brad?)

Be my tweetheart . . .

Now that I'm a celebrity (and one who's learned to write, at that), you can find me on Twitter. I've even got one of those little blue ticks to prove it's really me.

So if you've enjoyed reading my book, I'd love to hear from you. My Twitter name is @officialpudsey and if you follow me, you'll find all the latest news about what Ashleigh and I are up to as well as lots of other fun stuff. And why not use the hashtag #pudseybook to find other fans and join in the chat?

@officialpudsey
#pudseybook

When I can find a window in my busy schedule of sleeping, eating and tormenting Obi and Indi, I occasionally lift a paw and send a tweet too. You'll find witticisms, words of wisdom and updates on my attempts to perfect the worm at @handsomebradcat.* Accept no imitations. #catzrule

@handsomebradcat
#catzrule

*I'm still waiting for my blue tick. Who do I talk to about that?

Acknowledgements

It's come as a surprise to me that that I've reached a stage in my career where I can say I have 'people', but it's true. You'd like me to perform on stage or take a seat on the sofa of a chat show? That's fine. Talk to my people. I wouldn't be here without their support, encouragement and expertise, and so I'd like to thank them here.

I'll begin with Ashleigh, of course, who has shared my adventure from the start. This book is about her as much as me, and I hope I've made her proud. Then there's Penny and Grandma, who have rooted for us every step of the way, as have the pets and even a certain ginger tom from down the road. Thank you to Ashleigh's dad for being so patient and supportive, despite the fact that he's not really a 'dog' person. I don't think he realised how good I was at dancing until he watched our audition on TV – now he treats me like royalty and I can twist him round my little paw pad! Also thanks to Ashleigh's sister and brother, Tayla and Brett, who have been very understanding when family life was disrupted. Family and friends have all been there for us, and were incredible when it came to rounding up votes. I would also like to thank Wellingborough Dog Training Club where we train, for helping Ashleigh and me every step of the way on our journey. They are like our second family and have supported us in everything that we have accomplished.

Simon Cowell has been a star, also David Walliams,

Alesha Dixon and Amanda Holden as well as everyone who voted for me on *Britain's Got Talent*. Working behind the scenes, we have the management at ROAR Global – that's Jonathan Shalit and Nazli Alizadeh – and then the Syco team: Charles Garland, Nigel Hall, Liz Shaylor, Mark Brittain, Nicola Phillips and Ben Todd. On the literary side, I'd like to thank my publisher Adam Strange along with Hannah Boursnell, Marie Hrynczak and the rest of the team at Little, Brown for getting this book into your hands. And finally, I couldn't have done this without the help of Matt Whyman – my very own Doctor Doolittle.

Picture Credits